Primary Mathematics Intensive Practice is a series of 12 books written to provide challenging supplementary material for Singapore's Primary Mathematics,

The primary objective of this series of books is to help students generate greater interest in mathematics and gain more confidence in solving mathematical problems. To achieve this, special features are incorporated in the series.

SPECIAL FEATURES

Topical Review

Enables students of mixed abilities to be exposed to a good variety of questions which are of varying levels of difficulty so as to help them develop a better understanding of mathematical concepts and their applications.

Mid-Year or End-Of-Year Review

Provides students with a good review that summarizes the topics learned in Primary Mathematics.

Take the Challenge!

Deepens students' mathematical concepts and helps develop their mathematical reasoning and higher-order thinking skills as they practice their problem-solving strategies.

More Challenging Problems

Stimulate students' interest through challenging and thought-provoking problems which encourage them to think critically and creatively as they apply their knowledge and experience in solving these problems.

Why this Series?

Students will find this series of books a good complement and supplement to the Primary Mathematics textbooks and workbooks. The comprehensive coverage certainly makes this series a valuable resource for teachers, parents and tutors.

It is hoped that the special features in this series of books will inspire and spur young people to achieve better mathematical competency and greater mathematics problem-solving skills.

Published by
SingaporeMath.com Inc
404 Beavercreek Road #225
Oregon City, OR 97045
U.S.A.
E-mail: customerservice@singaporemath.com
www.singaporemath.com

First published 2004
Reprinted 2005
Reprinted 2006
Reprinted 2007
Reprinted 2008

ISBN 978-1-932906-01-1

Printed in Singapore

Our special thanks to Jenny Hoerst for her assistance in editing the U.S. edition of
Primary Mathematics Intensive Practice.

Primary 1B
Contents

Topic 1: Comparing Numbers

1. Fill in the blanks.

(a)

chicks	
frogs	

There are _____ more _____ than _____.

(b)

sea horses	
crabs	

There are _____ more _____ than _____.

(c)

bananas	
cherries	

There are _____ fewer _____ than _____.

2. Fill in the blanks.

   (a) 2 less than 8 is _____.

   (b) 8 more than 0 is _____.

   (c) 4 is 7 less than _____.

   (d) 15 is 5 more than _____.

   (e) 4 is _____ less than 16.

   (f) 11 is _____ more than 5.

   (g) _____ is 3 more than 9.

   (h) _____ is 10 less than 10.

   (i) 20 is _____ more than 8.

3. Look at the numbers in each set. Fill in the blank.

   (a) 12, 8, 16

   The smallest number is _____ less than the largest number.

   (b) 7, 9, 4, 10

   The largest number is _____ more than the smallest number.

   (c) 2, 4, 10, 11

   The smallest number is _____ less than 15.

   (d) 4, 9, 19, 11

   The _____ (largest, smallest) number is 11 more than 8.

WORD PROBLEMS

1. There are 5 roosters and 20 chickens. How many more chickens are there than roosters?

   There are _____ more chickens than roosters.

2. Nancy had 11 ribbons. Mary had 2 fewer ribbons than Nancy. How many ribbons does Mary have?

   Mary has _____ ribbons.

3. There are 14 birds on a fence. 2 flew away.

   (a) How many fewer birds are there now?

   (b) How many birds are left on the fence?

Take the Challenge!

1. There are 7 pears on the table and 3 apples.

   (a) How many more pears are there than apples?

   (b) Adam added two more apples. How many apples are there now?

   (c) How many more pears than apples are there now?

   (d) Adam then adds more apples so there are the same number of apples as pears. How many more apples does he add?

   (e) Then Mother puts 4 more pears and 6 more apples on the table. Are there more apples or pears now? How many more?

2.

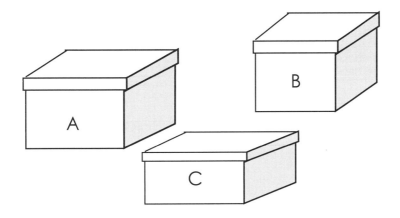

Boxes A, B, and C each contain some marbles.
Box A has 7 more marbles than Box B.
Box B has 5 fewer marbles than Box C.
Box C has 12 marbles.

How many marbles are there in Box A?

Topic 2: Picture Graphs

1. The picture graph below shows the favorite vegetable of some children. Each ☆ stands for 1 child.

Carrot	Broccoli	Tomato	Lettuce
☆ ☆ ☆ ☆ ☆ ☆ ☆ ☆	☆ ☆ ☆ ☆	☆ ☆ ☆ ☆ ☆ ☆	☆ ☆

Fill in the blanks.

(a) _____ children like carrots.

(b) _____ children like tomatoes.

(c) _____ more children like tomatoes than lettuce.

(d) _____ fewer children like broccoli than carrots.

(e) Two more children like broccoli than _____.

(f) Arrange the vegetables in order, starting from the favorite vegetable of most children.

_____ , _____ , _____ , _____

6

2. The picture graph below shows the favorite pets of some children. Each △ stands for 1 child.

| Dog | Horse | Cat | Monkey | Hamster | Rabbit |

Fill in the blanks.

(a) _____ children like rabbits.

(b) _____ children like cats.

(c) _____ children like dogs.

(d) _____ more children like cats than monkeys.

(e) _____ fewer children like horses than dogs.

(f) Five more children like dogs than _____.

(g) Three fewer children like rabbits than _____.

(h) There are _____ types of animals altogether.

(i) There are _____ horses, hamsters and rabbits altogether.

3. The picture graph below shows the number of different types of toys Sam has. Each ⬡ stands for 1 toy.

 Toy soldier	⬡ ⬡ ⬡ ⬡ ⬡ ⬡ ⬡ ⬡ ⬡ ⬡ ⬡
 Bear	⬡ ⬡ ⬡
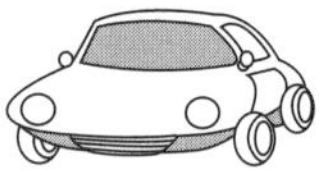 Toy car	⬡ ⬡ ⬡ ⬡ ⬡ ⬡ ⬡ ⬡ ⬡
 Marble	⬡ ⬡ ⬡ ⬡ ⬡ ⬡ ⬡ ⬡ ⬡ ⬡ ⬡ ⬡ ⬡ ⬡ ⬡
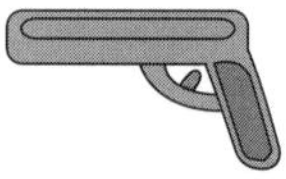 Toy gun	⬡ ⬡ ⬡ ⬡ ⬡ ⬡

Fill in the blanks.

(a) Sam has _____ toy soldiers.

(b) The number of toy guns Sam has is _____.

(c) Sam has _____ more marbles than toy cars.

(d) Sam has _____ fewer bears than toy soldiers.

(e) Sam has 3 more _____ than toy guns.

(f) Sam has 5 fewer toy soldiers than _____.

(g) Sam has _____ different types of toys altogether.

4. The picture graph below shows ice cream flavors children like. Each ☐ stands for 1 child.

Chocolate Fudge	☐☐☐☐☐☐☐☐☐☐
Caramel Swirl	☐☐
Mint Chocolate Chip	☐☐☐☐☐☐☐☐☐☐☐☐☐☐
Toffee	☐☐☐☐☐☐☐
Strawberry	☐☐☐☐☐
French Vanilla	☐☐☐☐☐☐☐☐☐

Fill in the blanks.

(a) _____ children like mint chocolate chip ice cream.

(b) _____ children like toffee ice cream.

(c) _____ more children like French vanilla ice cream than strawberry ice cream.

(d) _____ fewer children like toffee ice cream than chocolate fudge ice cream.

(e) Five more children like toffee ice cream than _____ .

(f) Four fewer children like _____ than mint chocolate chip.

(g) There are _____ children who like caramel swirl, toffee and chocolate fudge.

5. A class has 20 students. Five students like to collect stamps. Eight students like to collect stickers. Four students like to collect coins. The rest like to collect seashells.

(a) Complete the picture graph below. Each □ stands for 1 student.

Stamps	Stickers	Coins	Seashells

(b) Fill in the blank.

_____ students in the class like to collect seashells.

Take the Challenge!

This is a picture of a fruit stand.

 watermelon   cherry   mango

apple   tomato   papaya

strawberry   orange

Color the symbol of each fruit at the bottom of the picture graph. Then color the number of each type of fruit shown on the picture of the fruit stand. Each ◯ stands for 1 fruit.

Fill in the blanks.

(a) There are _____ oranges.

(b) There are _____ papayas.

(c) There are _____ watermelons.

(d) There are _____ tomatoes.

(e) There are _____ strawberries.

(f) There are _____ cherries.

(g) There are _____ apples.

(h) There are _____ mangoes.

(i) There are 5 more apples than _____.

(j) There are 10 fewer mangoes than _____.

(k) There are 9 more oranges than _____.

(l) There are 7 fewer watermelons than _____.

(m) There are 6 more tomatoes than _____.

(n) There are 8 fewer papayas than _____.

(o) There are _____ mangoes and papayas altogether.

(p) There are _____ watermelons and tomatoes altogether.

(q) There are _____ mangoes and watermelons altogether.

(r) There are _____ types of fruit altogether at the fruit stand.

Topic 3: Numbers to 40

1. Write down the correct number of items in each set.

(a)

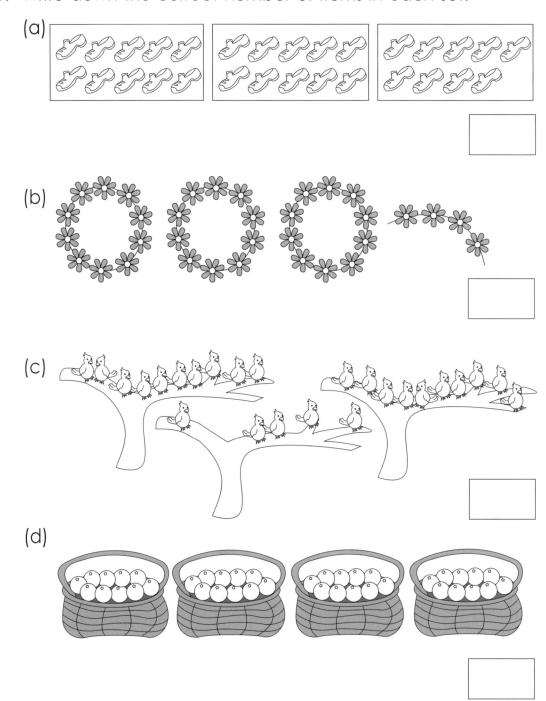

(b)

(c)

(d)

2. Color the item with the largest number and cross out (×) the item with the smallest number.

(a)

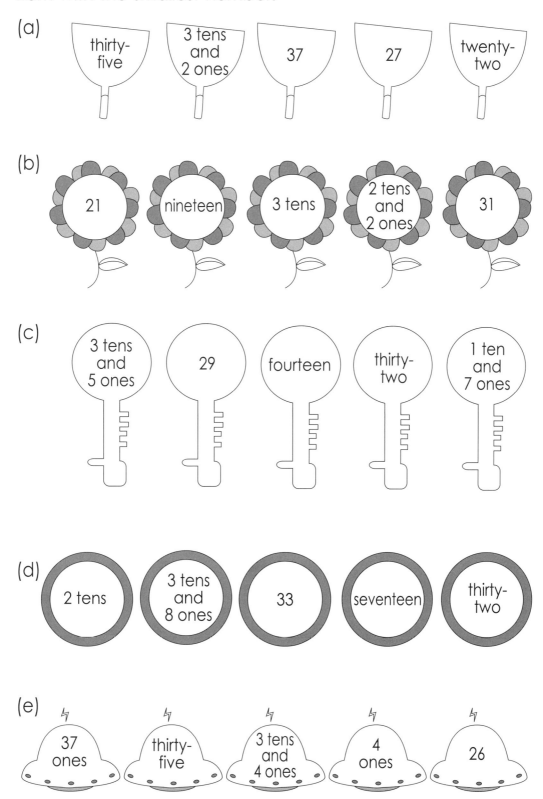

(b)

(c)

(d)

(e)

3. Fill in the blanks to complete the addition number sentences.

(a)

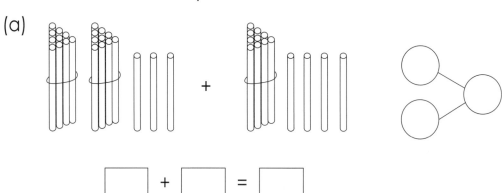

☐ + ☐ = ☐

(b)

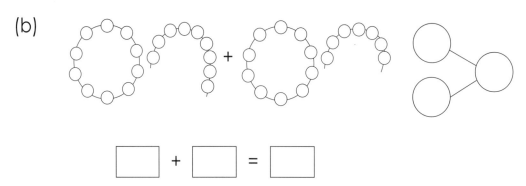

☐ + ☐ = ☐

(c)

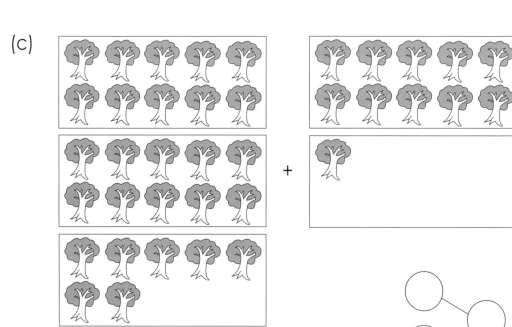

☐ + ☐ = ☐

4. Add by 'counting on'.

   Example: 23 + 4 = <u>27</u>
   Count 4 ones from 23:   24, 25, 26, <u>27</u>

   (a) 19 + 5 = _____

   (b) 27 + 4 = _____

   (c) 33 + 2 = _____

   (d) 21 + 3 = _____

   (e) 35 + 4 = _____

   (f) 20 + 8 = _____

   (g) 22 + 5 = _____

   (h) 34 + 3 = _____

5. Add using number bonds.

   Example: 24 + 5 = <u>29</u>

   Step 1:   24 + 5

   Step 2:   Add 5 to 4.
                   4 + 5 = 9

   Step 3:   20 + 9 = 29

   Step 4:   24 + 5 = <u>29</u>

   Add using by making tens.

   Example: 27 + 6 = <u>33</u>

   Step 1:   27 + 6

                   ③   ③

   Step 2:   Add 3 to 27.
                   27 + 3 = 30

   Step 3:   30 + 3 = 33

   Step 4:   27 + 6 = <u>33</u>

(a)   22 + 6 = _____

(b)   31 + 8 = _____

(c)   25 + 9 = _____

(d)   5 + 26 = _____

(e)   29 + 7 = _____

(f)   27 + 8 = _____

(g)   26 + 4 = _____

(h)   6 + 28 = _____

6. Adding 3 numbers.

Example: 7 + 6 + 8 = 21

Step 1:   Add 7 and 6 first.
               7 + 6 = 13

Step 2:   Add 13 and 8 next.
               13 + 8 = 21

Add the numbers on each line and write the answer in the
    box at the end of the line.

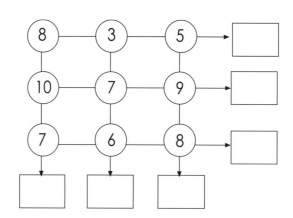

7. Do the addition number sentences on the toy plane. Match the answers with the colors given, then color the toy plane.

24 – green   37 – red   29 – blue
33 – orange   40 – yellow   31 – purple

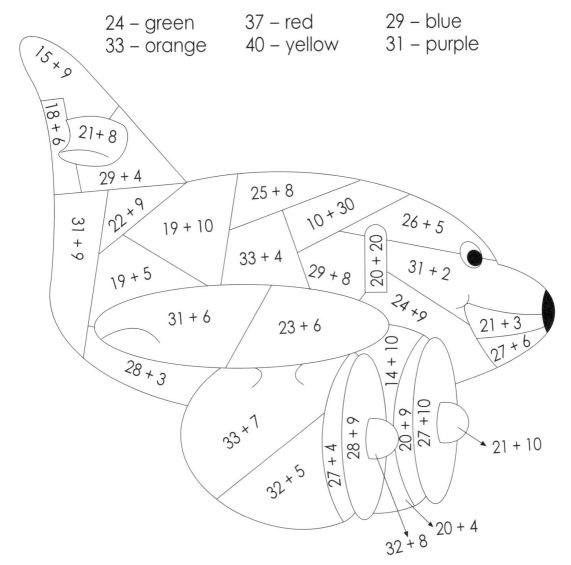

8. Subtract by 'counting backwards'.

Example: 36 – 3 = <u>33</u>
Count 4 ones backwards from 36:   35, 34, <u>33</u>

(a) 37 – 2 = _____   (b) 25 – 4 = _____

(c) 21 – 5 = _____   (d) 30 – 6 = _____

(e) 31 – 3 = _____   (f) 28 – 5 = _____

(g) 22 – 4 = _____   (h) 40 – 3 = _____

9. Subtract using number bonds.

Example: 37 – 4 = <u>33</u>

Step 1:   37 – 4

       (30) (7)

Step 2:   Subtract 4 from 7.
            7 – 4 = 3

Step 3:   30 + 3 = 33

Step 4:   37 – 4 = <u>33</u>

Subtract using number bonds.

Example: 21 – 5 = <u>16</u>

Step 1:   21 – 5

       (11) (10)

Step 2:   Subtract 5 from 10.
            10 – 5 = 5

Step 3:   11 + 5 = 16

Step 4:   21 – 5 = <u>16</u>

(a)   25 – 3 = _____

(b)   39 – 5 = _____

(c)   23 – 8 = _____

(d)   32 – 7 = _____

(e)   40 – 9 = _____

(f)   37 – 6 = _____

(g)   28 – 7 = _____

(h)   24 – 9 = _____

10. Fill in the missing numbers. The first one has been done for you.

(a)

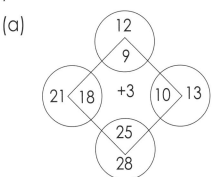

(b)

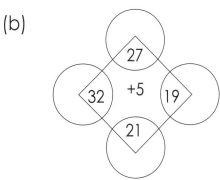

(c)

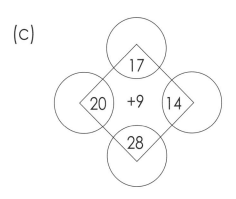

(d)

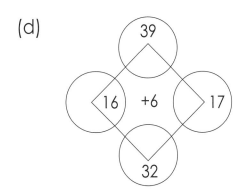

(e)

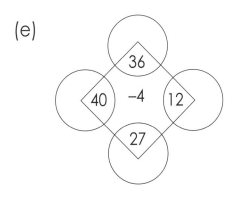

(f)

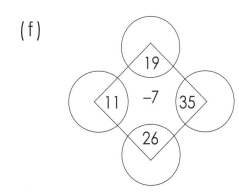

(g)

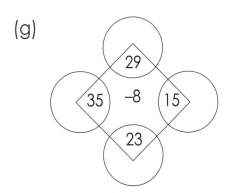

(h)

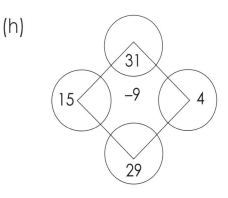

11. Check (✓) the correct statements and cross out (✗) the wrong statements.

   (a) 35 is the same as 3 tens and 3 ones.   (   )

   (b) 2 tens and 9 ones make 29.   (   )

   (c) 4 ones make 40.   (   )

   (d) 3 tens and 4 ones is more than 30 ones.   (   )

   (e) 27 is less than 2 tens and 5 ones.   (   )

   (f) 31 is 8 less than 37.   (   )

   (g) 4 less than 27 is larger than 20.   (   )

   (h) 7 more than 31 is less then 38.   (   )

   (i) 9 less than 40 is equal to 6 more than 29.   (   )

   (j) 5 more than 28 is larger than 3 tens.   (   )

WORD PROBLEMS

1. Kelly has 25 straws. Her brother takes away 7 of her straws. How many straws does Kelly have left?

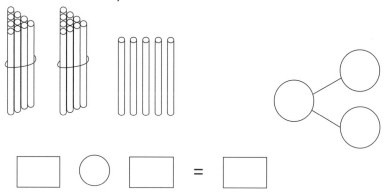

Kelly has _____ straws left.

22

2. There are 31 students in a class. Five new students join the class. How many students are there in the class now?

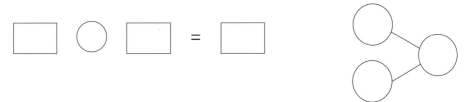

There are _____ students in the class now.

3. There are 37 cans of drink in a store. The storekeeper sold 8 cans. How many cans of drink are left in the store?

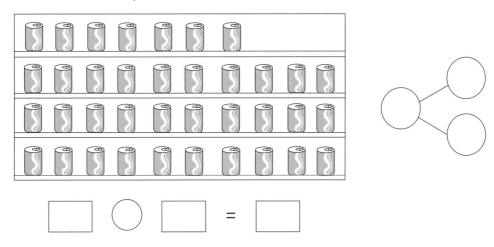

_____ cans of drink are left in the store.

4. Shirley has 19 coins. Dennis has 6 coins and Evelyn has 8 coins. How many coins do they have altogether?

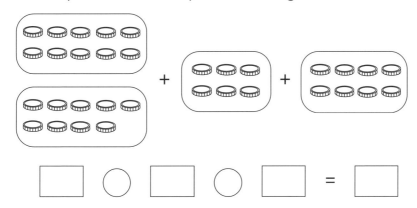

They have _____ coins altogether.

23

5. Mark is on Level 34 of a building. How many levels does he have to go down to reach Level 28 of the building?

$$\boxed{} \bigcirc \boxed{} = \boxed{}$$

He has to go down _____ levels to reach Level 28.

6. There are 23 people in Bus A. There are 31 people in Bus B.

   (a) Which bus has more people?

   Bus _____ has more people.

   (b) How many more people?

   $$\boxed{} \bigcirc \boxed{} = \boxed{}$$

   There are _____ more people.

7. There were 26 apples on an apple tree. Josh picked 5 apples from the tree. Sally picked 8 apples. How many apples are left on the tree?

$$\boxed{} \bigcirc \boxed{} \bigcirc \boxed{} = \boxed{}$$

_____ apples are left on the tree.

24

8. Adelyn has 10 ribbons. Beatrice has 9 more ribbons than Adelyn. How many ribbons does Beatrice have?

$$\boxed{} \bigcirc \boxed{} = \boxed{}$$

Beatrice has _____ ribbons.

9. There are 18 children in line. Mike and Terry join the line. Then, another group of 7 children joins the line. How many children are there in line altogether?

$$\boxed{} \bigcirc \boxed{} \bigcirc \boxed{} = \boxed{}$$

There are _____ children in line altogether.

Take the Challenge!

1. Study the patterns. FInd the missing numbers.

(a)

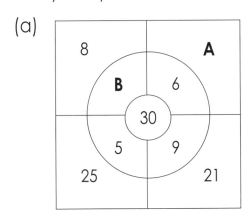

A = _____

B = _____

(b)

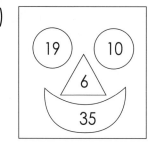

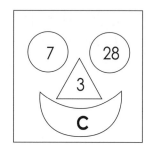

C = _____

2. If $\triangledown$ + ☐ = 9

and $\triangledown$ + $\triangledown$ + ☐ = 15

then $\triangledown$ = _____

and ☐ = _____

Topic 4: Multiplication

1. Fill in the missing numbers.

(a)

☐ + ☐ + ☐ + ☐ = ☐

☐ × ☐ = ☐

(b)

☐ + ☐ + ☐ + ☐ + ☐ = ☐

☐ × ☐ = ☐

(c)

☐ + ☐ + ☐ + ☐ = ☐

☐ × ☐ = ☐

(d)

☐ + ☐ + ☐ = ☐

☐ × ☐ = ☐

(e)

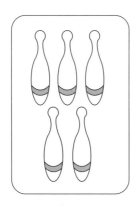 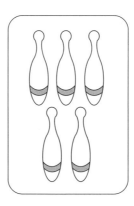 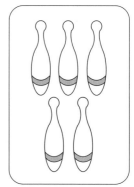

☐ + ☐ + ☐ = ☐

☐ × ☐ = ☐

2. Match the correct number to the correct picture. Then fill in the correct answers. The first one has been done for you.

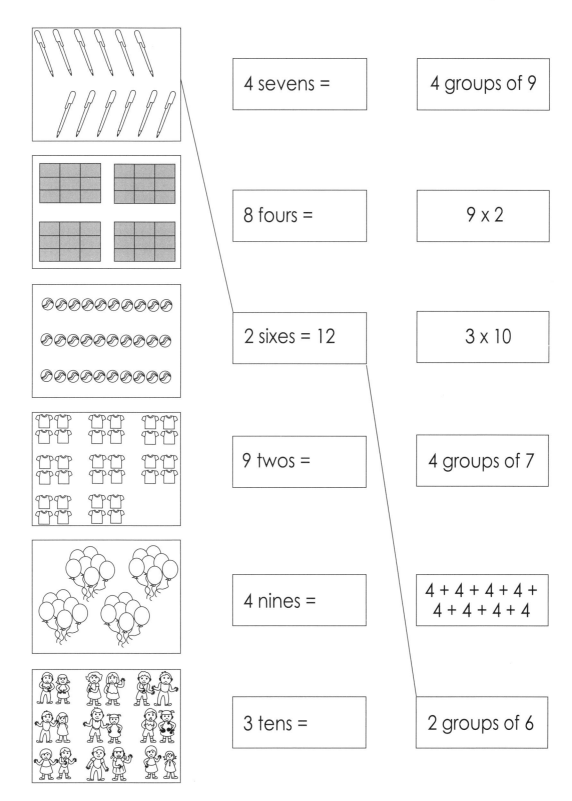

4 sevens =

4 groups of 9

8 fours =

9 x 2

2 sixes = 12

3 x 10

9 twos =

4 groups of 7

4 nines =

4 + 4 + 4 + 4 + 4 + 4 + 4 + 4

3 tens =

2 groups of 6

3. Fill in the missing numbers.

(a)

$$\boxed{} \times \boxed{} = \boxed{}$$

(b)

$$\boxed{} \times \boxed{} = \boxed{}$$

(c)

$$\boxed{} \times \boxed{} = \boxed{}$$

(d)

$$\boxed{} \times \boxed{} = \boxed{}$$

(e)

$$\boxed{} \times \boxed{} = \boxed{}$$

4. Draw the correct number of ☆ in each oval to show 4 × 7. Then fill in the missing numbers in the boxes.

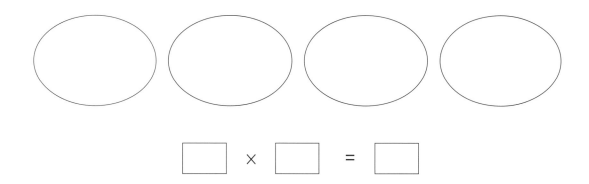

☐ × ☐ = ☐

5. Draw the correct number of ☐ in each oval to show 8 × 2. Then fill in the missing numbers in the boxes.

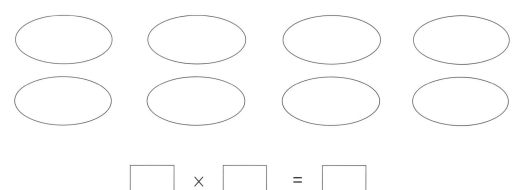

☐ × ☐ = ☐

6. Draw the correct number of ♡ in each oval to show 3 × 9. Then fill in the missing numbers in the boxes.

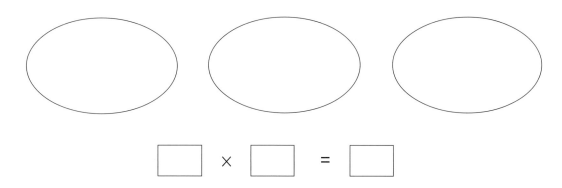

☐ × ☐ = ☐

7. Draw the correct number of ◇ in each oval to show 10 × 4. Then fill in the missing numbers in the boxes.

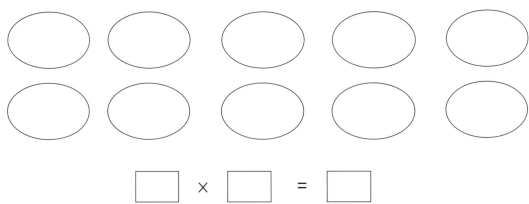

☐ × ☐ = ☐

8. Draw the correct number of △ in each oval to show 7 × 5. Then fill in the missing numbers in the boxes.

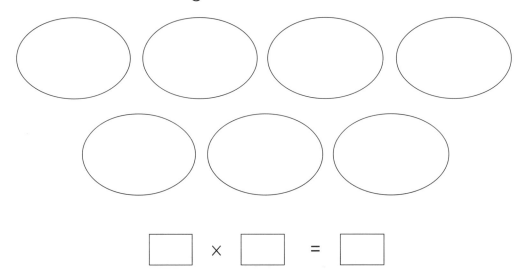

☐ × ☐ = ☐

9. Check (✓) the correct statements and cross out (✗) the wrong statements.

   (a) 7 × 5 is equal to 5 + 5 + 5 + 5 + 5.   (   )

   (b) 0 × 1 is equal to 1.   (   )

   (c) 6 groups of 5 is the same as 5 × 6.   (   )

(d) 7 fours is larger than 4 × 7.   (   )

(e) One horse has 4 legs. Four horses have
    4 + 4 + 4 + 4 legs.   (   )

(f) 4 × 5 is not the same as 4 + 5.   (   )

(g) 9 + 9 + 9 + 9 is less than 9 groups of 3.   (   )

(h) 10 + 10 is larger than 10 twos.   (   )

(i) 1 girl has 10 dolls. 3 girls have
    3 + 3 + 3 + 3 + 3 + 3 + 3 + 3 + 3 dolls.   (   )

(j) 8 groups of 3 is larger than 2 × 8.   (   )

10. Fill in the missing number(s) in each pattern.

(a)

(b)

(c)

(d)

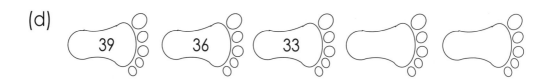

(e)

WORD PROBLEMS

1. Mother bought some cakes. She packed them in boxes of 8 for each of her 4 children. How many cakes did Mother buy?

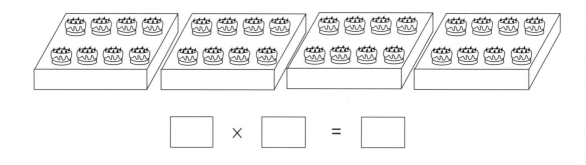

$$\boxed{} \times \boxed{} = \boxed{}$$

She bought _____ cakes.

2. Manuel has 6 cups. He puts 3 eggs into each cup. How many eggs are there altogether?

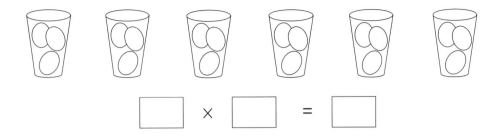

$$\boxed{} \times \boxed{} = \boxed{}$$

There are _____ eggs altogether.

3. Sarah buys 5 bags of chocolate. Each bag contains 6 pieces of chocolate. How many pieces of chocolate does Sarah have?

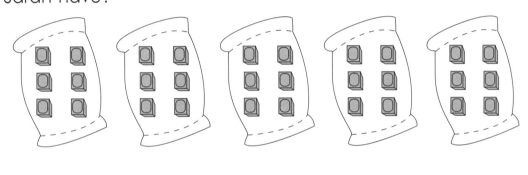

$$\boxed{} \times \boxed{} = \boxed{}$$

Sarah has _____ pieces of chocolate.

4.

(a) There are _____ dancing elephants.

(b) Each dancing elephant has _____ legs.

(c) There are _____ legs altogether.

5. Kelson has 3 strings of 7 seashells each. Lynn has 2 strings of 7 seashells each. How many seashells do they have altogether?

Kelson: [ ] × [ ] = [ ]

Lynn: [ ] × [ ] = [ ]

[ ] + [ ] = [ ]

They have _____ seashells altogether.

6. Tommy has 3 bags of candy. Each bag had 10 pieces of candy. Tommy ate 7 pieces of candy. How many pieces of candy did Tommy have left?

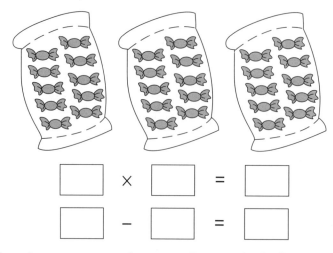

[ ] × [ ] = [ ]

[ ] − [ ] = [ ]

Tommy had _____ pieces of candy left.

7. There are 5 birds in a cage. Two more birds are added to the cage. How many wings are there in the cage altogether?

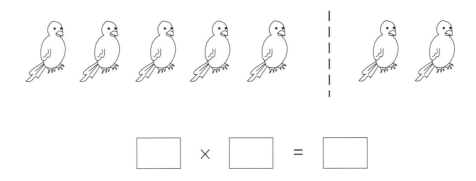

$$\boxed{} \times \boxed{} = \boxed{}$$

There are _____ wings in the cage altogether.

8. (a) Samantha, Kelly and Mollie put their feet together. How many toes are there altogether?

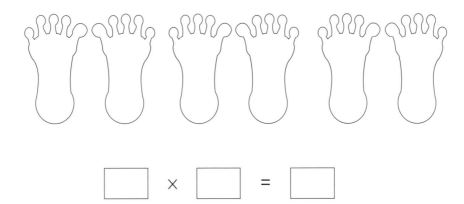

$$\boxed{} \times \boxed{} = \boxed{}$$

There are _____ toes altogether.

(b) Kelly covers up 8 of her toes. How many toes are left?

$$\boxed{} - \boxed{} = \boxed{}$$

_____ toes are left.

Take the Challenge!

Fill in the blanks with the given words.

greater than,   less than,   the same as

(a) 8×6 is _____ $8 + 8 + 8 + 8 + 8$.

(b) 2×9 is _____ $9 + 9 + 9$

but _____ $2 + 2 + 2 + 2 + 2 + 2 + 2$.

(c) $5 + 5 + 5 + 5$ is _____ 4×5.

(d) 10×7 is _____ $10 + 10 + 10 + 10 + 10 + 10 + 10$

which is _____ $10 + 10 + 8 + 8 + 8 + 8 + 8$.

(e) $9 + 9 + 9 + 10$ is _____ 4×9.

Topic 5: Division

1. Circle correctly. Then fill in the blanks.

   (a) Group the chairs by circling them into sets of 3.

   There are _____ sets of 3 chairs.

   (b) Group the rats by circling them into sets of 4.

   There are _____ sets of 4 rats.

   (c) Group the dolls by circling them into sets of 2.

   There are _____ sets of 2 dolls.

   (d) Group the carrots by circling them into sets of 7.

   There are _____ sets of 7 carrots.

2. Circle correctly. Then fill in the blanks.

(a) Put 15 strawberries equally into 5 groups.

There are _____ strawberries in each group.

(b) Put 20 mangoes equally into 4 groups.

There are _____ mangoes in each group.

(c) Put 16 apples equally into 8 groups.

There are _____ apples in each group.

(d) Put 18 watermelons equally into 3 groups.

There are _____ watermelons in each group.

3. Circle correctly. Then fill in the blanks.

(a) Put the eggs equally into the bowls by circling them.

There are _____ eggs altogether.

There are _____ bowls.

There are _____ eggs in each bowl.

(b) Put the tarts equally onto the plates by circling them.

There are _____ tarts altogether.

There are _____ plates.

There are _____ tarts on each plate.

(c) Put the balls equally into the buckets by circling them.

There are _____ balls altogether.

There are _____ buckets.

There are _____ balls in each bucket.

4. Circle correctly. Then fill in the blanks.

(a) Share the pieces of candy equally among the children by circling them.

There are _____ pieces of candy altogether.

There are _____ children.

Each child gets _____ pieces of candy.

(b) Feed the cats with an equal number of cans of food by circling them.

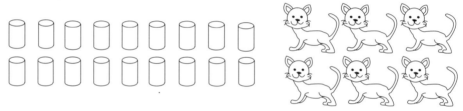

There are _____ cans of food altogether.

There are _____ cats.

Each cat gets _____ cans of food.

(c) Share the dresses equally among the girls by circling them.

There are _____ dresses altogether.

There are _____ girls.

Each girl gets _____ dresses.

WORD PROBLEMS

1. Aaron puts 15 toys equally into some boxes. If each box has 3 toys, how many boxes are there?

There are _____ boxes.

2. Mr. Brown bought 12 toy cars and gave 3 toy cars to each of his sons. How many sons does Mr. Brown have?

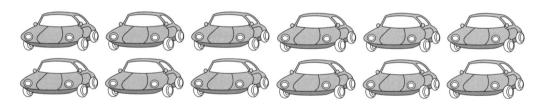

Mr. Brown has _____ sons.

3. Sally has 16 cherries. If she wants to put 8 cherries on 1 cake, how many cakes will she need?

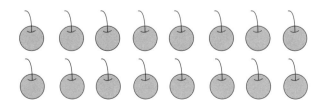

She will need _____ cakes.

4. There are 18 children at a party. Three equal groups are formed. How many children are there in each group?

There are _____ children in each group.

5. I bought 20 muffins. I ate 4 muffins and gave the rest equally to my 4 sisters. How many muffins did each of my sisters get?

Each of my sisters got _____ muffins.

6. There are 14 dogs playing in a park. Two more dogs join them. If we put all the dogs into 8 equal groups, how many dogs will there be in each group?

There will be _____ dogs in each group.

7. Mary and Lucy each have 6 lollipops. Amy has 3 lollipops. They decide to share their lollipops equally among themselves. How many lollipops will each girl get?

Each girl will get _____ lollipops.

8. There are 18 spiders on a web. Five spiders crawled away from the web. Another new spider crawled onto the web. If the spiders on the web are to be put into 2 groups equally, how many spiders will there be in each group?

There will be _____ spiders in each group.

Take the Challenge!

1. Kathy has 3 strings of pearls. Each string has 6 pearls. She wants to re-string the pearls by using 2 strings only. How many pearls will there be in each string?

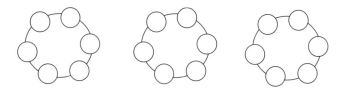

There will be _____ pearls in each string.

2. Draw more oranges so that 4 oranges can be put on each of the plates.

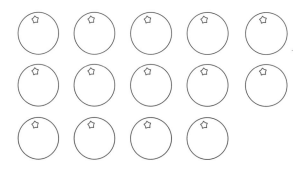

Topic 6: Time

1. Match the clocks to the correct time.

(a)

9 o'clock

Half past 9

(b)

Half past 8

Half past 11

(c)

8 o'clock

(d)

5 o'clock

11 o'clock

(e)

Half past 2

Half past 1

(f)

1 o'clock

2. Write the time shown on each clock.

(a)

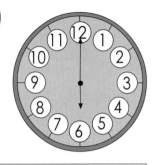

(b)

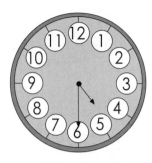

(c)

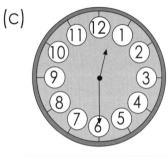

(d)

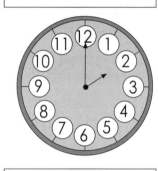

(e)

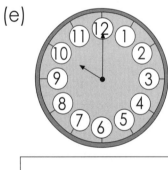

(f)

(g)

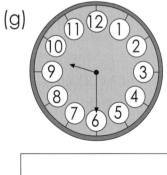

(h)

3. Tell the time in each case.

(a)
Kenneth was eating his breakfast at _____.

(b)
Mrs. Marshall was cooking lunch at _____.

(c)
Mr. Palmer was having his coffee break at _____.

(d)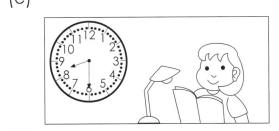
Matthew's family was having dinner at _____.

(e)
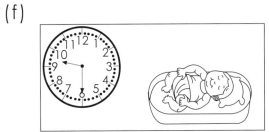
Cecilia was doing her homework at _____.

(f)

Baby Jonathan was already asleep by _____.

4. Draw the hour hand on each clock face to show the time.

(a)

| 5 o'clock |

(b)

| 8 o'clock |

(c)

| Half past 3 |

(d)

| 12 o'clock |

(e)

| Half past 7 |

(f)

| Half past 6 |

5. Draw the minute hand on each clock face to show the time.

(a)

| 7 o'clock |

(b)

| Half past 5 |

(c)

| 3 o'clock |

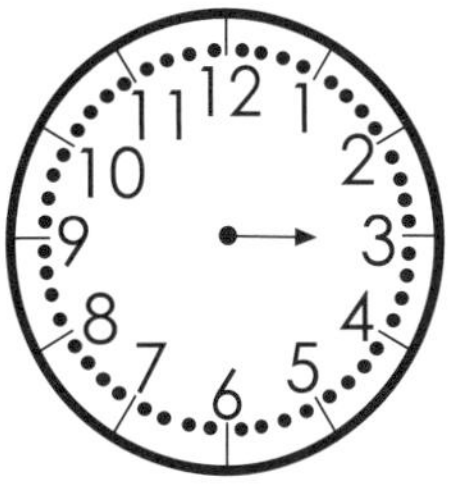

(d)

| 11 o'clock |

(e)

| Half past 11 |

(f)

| 12 o'clock |

6. Look at the time and draw the missing hour hand or minute hand.

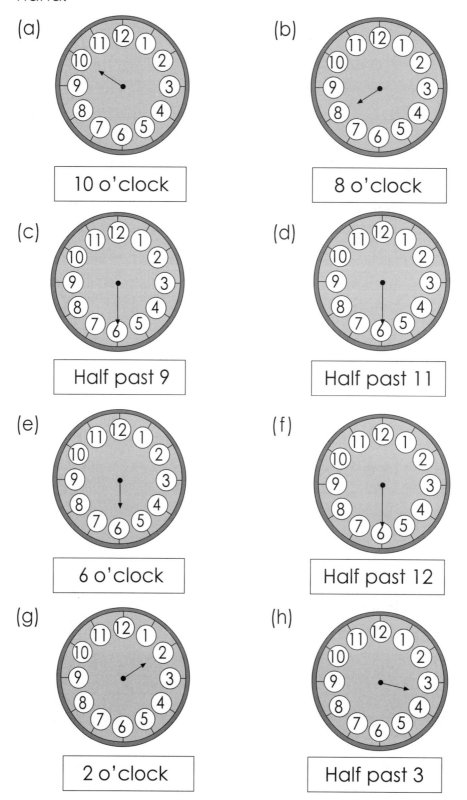

(a)

10 o'clock

(b)

8 o'clock

(c)

Half past 9

(d)

Half past 11

(e)

6 o'clock

(f)

Half past 12

(g)

2 o'clock

(h)

Half past 3

Take the Challenge!

Draw the missing hour hand and minute hand on the last clock to complete each pattern.

(a)

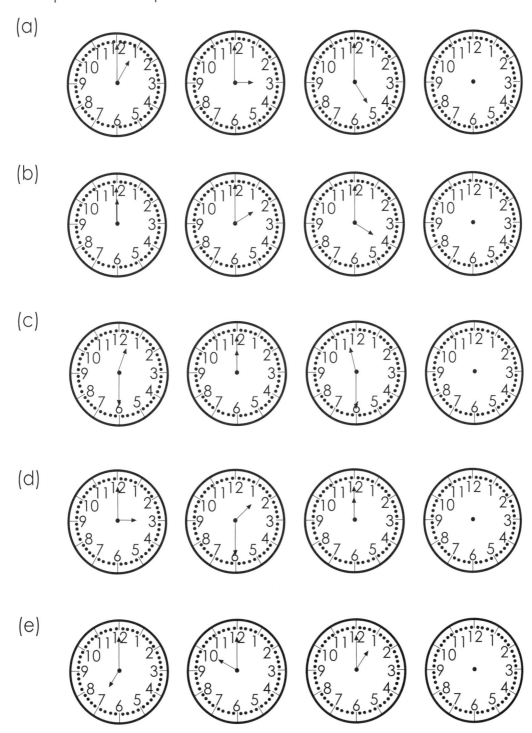

(b)

(c)

(d)

(e)

1. Count the number of items and write the correct number in words.

(a)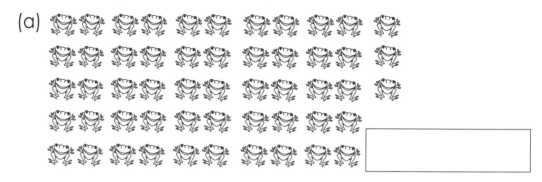

(b)

(c)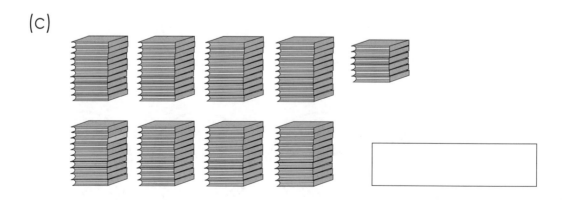

(d)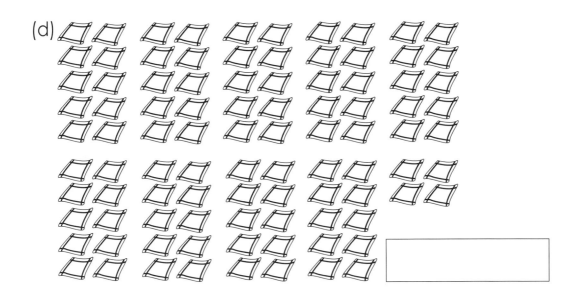

2. Fill in the blanks.

(a) 4 tens and 6 ones = _____

(b) 7 tens and 3 ones = _____

(c) 49 = _____ tens and _____ ones

(d) 85 = _____ tens and _____ ones

(e) 90 = _____ ones

(f) 38 ones = _____ tens and _____ ones

(g) 54 = _____ ones

(h) 7 ones + 8 ones = _____ ten(s) _____ ones

                       = _____

(i) 3 ones + 6 ones = _____

(j) 3 tens + 6 tens = _____

(k) 8 ones – 5 ones = _____

(l) 8 tens – 5 tens = _____

3. Color the train carriage with the largest number and cross out (✘) the train carriage with the smallest number.

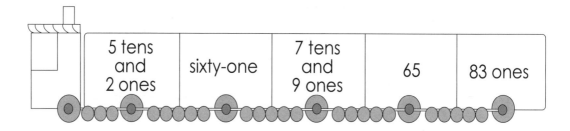

| 5 tens and 2 ones | sixty-one | 7 tens and 9 ones | 65 | 83 ones |

4. Color the balloon with the smallest number and circle the balloon with the largest number.

| 6 tens and 7 ones | 87 | ninety -five | 9 tens and 3 ones | nineteen |

5. Arrange the television sets, starting from the largest number.

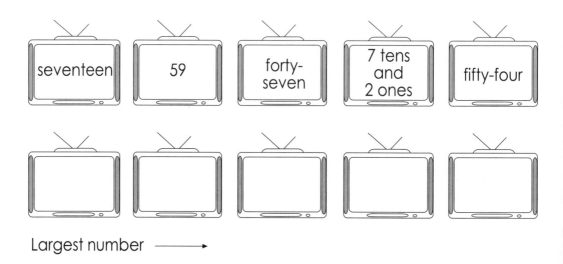

| seventeen | 59 | forty- seven | 7 tens and 2 ones | fifty-four |

Largest number ⟶

6. Add by 'counting on'.

Example 1: 78 + 3 = 81
Count 3 ones from 78: 79, 80, 81

Example 2: 65 + 30 = 95
Count 3 tens from 65: 75, 85, 95

(a) 43 + 4 = _____   (b) 51 + 6 = _____

(c) 36 + 50 = _____   (d) 20 + 48 = _____

(e) 72 + 3 = _____   (f) 5 + 81 = _____

(g) 44 + 30 = _____   (h) 68 + 3 = _____

(i) 29 + 40 = _____   (j) 93 + 5 = _____

7. Add ones using number bonds.

Example: 54 + 3 = 57

Step 1: 54 + 3

Step 2: Add 3 to 4.
4 + 3 = 7

Step 3: 50 + 7 = 57

Step 4: 54 + 3 = 57

Add ones by making tens.

Example: 48 + 7 = 55

Step 1: 48 + 7

2   5

Step 2: Add 2 to 48
48 + 2 = 50

Step 3: 50 + 5 = 55

Step 4: 48 + 7 = 55

(a) 63 + 6 = _____

(b) 85 + 8 = _____

(c) 72 + 7 = _____

(d) 9 + 55 = _____

(e) 44 + 6 = _____

(f) 5 + 92 = _____

(g) 57 + 4 = _____

(h) 81 + 7 = _____

(i) 68 + 6 = _____

(j) 8 + 75 = _____

8. Add tens using number bonds.

   Example: 62 + 30 = <u>92</u>

   Step 1:   62 + 30

   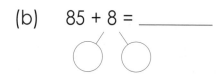

   Step 2:   Add 30 to 60.
               60 + 30 = 90

   Step 3:   90 + 2 = 92

   Step 4:   62 + 30 = <u>92</u>

   (a) 45 + 50 = _____

   (b) 33 + 60 = _____

   (c) 79 + 20 = _____

   (d) 56 + 30 = _____

(e)   40 + 27 = _____   (f)   48 + 40 = _____

9. Add tens and ones.

Example: 52 + 39 = <u>91</u>

Step 1:   52 +   39

Step 2:   Add the tens.
52 + 30 = 82

Step 3:   Then add the ones.
82 + 9 = 91

Step 4:   52 + 39 = <u>91</u>

(a)   24 +   63 = _____   (b)   18 +   57 = _____

(c)   49 +   26 = _____   (d)   35 +   12 = _____

(e)   71 +   13 = _____   (f)   38 +   42 = _____

(g)   26 +   51 = _____   (h)   65 +   19 = _____

(i)   66 +   17 = _____   (j)   34 +   22 = _____

10. Look for a pattern and fill in the missing numbers.

(a)

(b)

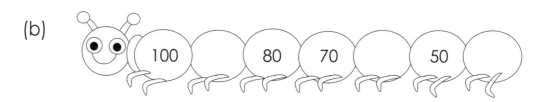

(c)

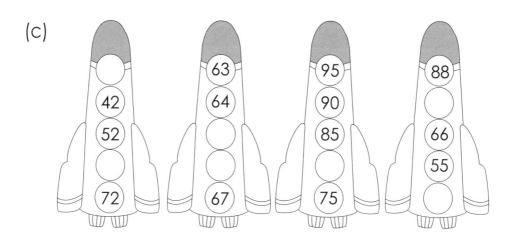

(d)

11. Subtract by 'counting backwards'.

Example 1: 73 – 4 = <u>69</u>
Count 4 ones backwards from 73:   72, 71, 70, <u>69</u>

Example 2: 65 – 30 = <u>35</u>
Count 3 tens backwards from 65:   55, 45, <u>35</u>

(a) 53 – 5 = _____

(b) 81 – 3 = _____

(c) 78 – 40 = _____

(d) 95 – 30 = _____

(e) 62 – 4 = _____

(f) 77 – 20 = _____

(g) 49 – 2 = _____

(h) 60 – 5 = _____

(i) 87 – 50 = _____

(j) 73 – 60 = _____

12. Subtract ones using number bonds.

Example: 87 – 5 = <u>82</u>

Step 1:   87 – 5

  (80)   (7)

Step 2:   Subtract 5 from 7.
              7 – 5 = 2

Step 3:   80 + 2 = 82

Step 4:   87 – 5 = <u>82</u>

  Subtract ones by subtracting from a ten.

Example: 63 – 6 = <u>57</u>

Step 1:   63 – 6

  (53)   (10)

Step 2:   Subtract 6 from 10.
              10 – 6 = 4

Step 3:   53 + 4 = 57

Step 4:   63 – 6 = <u>57</u>

(a)   58 – 6 = _____

(b)   75 – 3 = _____

(c)   61 – 7 = _____   (d)   43 – 5 = _____

(e)   89 – 8 = _____   (f)   62 – 6 = _____

(g)   80 – 9 = _____   (h)   59 – 5 = _____

(i)   77 – 8 = _____   (j)   96 – 4 = _____

13. Subtract tens using number bonds.

Example: 94 – 30 = <u>64</u>

Step 1:   94 – 30

4   90

Step 2:   Subtract 30 from 90.
90 – 30 = 60

Step 3:   60 + 4 = 64

Step 4:   94 – 30 = <u>64</u>

(a)   46 – 20 = _____   (b)   59 – 40 = _____

(c)   85 – 30 = _____   (d)   67 – 50 = _____

(e)   93 – 40 = _____   (f)   71 – 20 = _____

○ ○   ○ ○

14. Subtract tens and ones.

Example: 76 – 34 = 42

Step 1:   76 –   34

               30   4

Step 2:   Subtract the tens.
             76 – 30 = 46

Step 3:   Then subtract the ones.
             46 – 4 = 42

Step 4:   76 – 32 = 42

   Subtract tens and ones using number bonds.

Example: 92 – 27 = 65

Step 1:   92 –   27

               20   7

Step 2:   Subtract the tens.
             92 – 20 = 62

Step 3:   Then subtract the ones.
             62 – 7 = 65

Step 4:   92 – 27 = 65

(a)   68 –   35 = _____   (b)   75 –   24 = _____

○ ○   ○ ○

63

(c)   94   –   18 = _____   (d)   49   –   27 = _____

(e)   60   –   15 = _____   (f)   51   –   16 = _____

(g)   83   –   47 = _____   (h)   57   –   49 = _____

(i)   77   –   31 = _____   (j)   86   –   22 = _____

15. Check (✓) the correct statements and cross out (✗) the wrong statements.

   (a) 7 tens and 6 ones make 76.   (   )

   (b) Add 40 to 41, the answer is less than 80 ones.   (   )

   (c) Take 9 away from 92, the answer is 86.   (   )

   (d) 83 is the same as 77 ones and 6 ones.   (   )

   (e) 45 + 34 is larger than 56 + 33.   (   )

   (f) 20 + 40 gives 6 tens.   (   )

   (g) 76 – 8 is less than 90 – 33.   (   )

   (h) Take 14 away from 80, the answer is
        larger than 70 + 3.   (   )

   (i) 89 is larger than 64 + 9 but less than 60 + 21.   (   )

WORD PROBLEMS

1. Margaret has 38 stamps. Her sister has 17 more stamps than her. How many stamps does Margaret's sister have?

$$\boxed{} \bigcirc \boxed{} = \boxed{}$$

Margaret's sister has _____ stamps.

2. Mike bought 57 marbles. On his way home, he lost 14 marbles. Later, he gave 19 marbles to his cousin. How many marbles did Mike have left?

$$\boxed{} \bigcirc \boxed{} = \boxed{}$$

$$\boxed{} \bigcirc \boxed{} = \boxed{}$$

Mike had _____ marbles left.

3. I have 25 pieces of chocolate. Monica has 17 pieces of chocolate more than I. How many pieces of chocolate do we have altogether?

$$\boxed{} \bigcirc \boxed{} = \boxed{}$$

$$\boxed{} \bigcirc \boxed{} = \boxed{}$$

We have _____ pieces of chocolate altogether.

4. There were 44 eggs in the house before Monday. On Monday, 15 eggs were eaten. On Tuesday, 23 more eggs were bought. How many eggs were left in the house after Tuesday?

☐ ◯ ☐ = ☐

☐ ◯ ☐ = ☐

_____ eggs were left in the house after Tuesday.

5. Jason is 42 years old. Maggie is 19 years younger than Jason. How old is Maggie?

☐ ◯ ☐ = ☐

Maggie is _____ years old.

6.

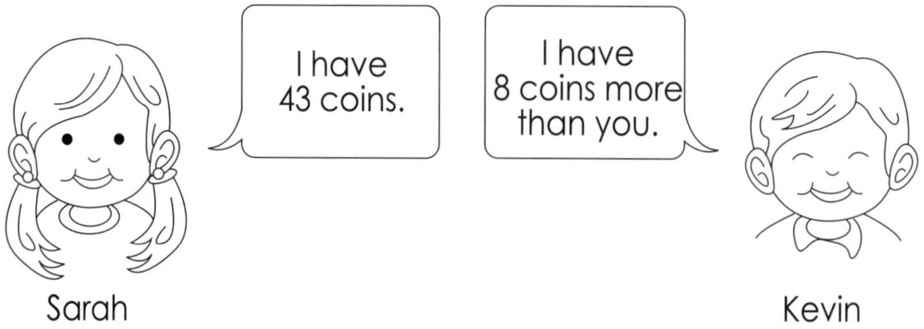

I have 43 coins.

I have 8 coins more than you.

Sarah

Kevin

How many coins does Kevin have?

☐ ◯ ☐ = ☐

Kevin has _____ coins.

7. Bag A has 57 potatoes. Bag B has 38 potatoes.

(a) How many more potatoes are there in Bag A than Bag B?

$\boxed{} \bigcirc \boxed{} = \boxed{}$

There are _____ more potatoes in Bag A than Bag B.

(b) How many potatoes are there altogether?

$\boxed{} \bigcirc \boxed{} = \boxed{}$

There are _____ potatoes altogether.

8. The number of marbles inside the box is 30 more than the number of marbles outside the box. How many marbles are there in the box?

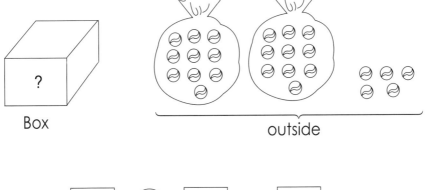

Box   outside

$\boxed{} \bigcirc \boxed{} = \boxed{}$

There are _____ marbles in the box.

Take the Challenge!

1. Can you list all the different ways to group 68 straws into tens and ones?
   List them by filling in the numbers in the boxes below. The first one has been done for you.

68 = [6] tens [8] ones

= [   ] tens [   ] ones

= [   ] tens [   ] ones

= [   ] tens [   ] ones

= [   ] tens [   ] ones

= [   ] ten [   ] ones

2. Look for a pattern. Find each missing number.

(a)
20	40		60	10		50	10		10	30
30	10		10	20		20	20		50	?

The missing number is _____.

(b)
2	9	16
?	18	25

The missing number is _____.

68

Topic 8: Money

1. Fill in the blanks.

(a) (10¢) = _____ nickels

(b) (25¢) = _____ pennies

(c) (25¢) = _____ nickels

(d) | $1 | = _____ dimes

(e) | $5 | = _____ one-dollar bills

(f) | $10 | = _____ one-dollar bills

(g) | $10 | = _____ five-dollar bills

(h) | $20 | = _____ ten-dollar bills

(i) | $20 | = _____ five-dollar bills

(j) | $100 | = _____ ten-dollar bills

2. Count and match to the correct amount.

(a)
25¢	25¢	10¢
5¢	10¢	1¢ 1¢

$39

70¢

(b)
25¢	25¢	1¢
	5¢	1¢ 1¢
10¢	1¢	1¢

97¢

$38

(c)
$1	$10
$5	$5
$1	$1

77¢

$25

(d)
25¢	25¢	5¢	1¢
10¢	1¢	1¢	25¢

78¢

$23

(e)
$5	$20
$1	$1
$1	$10

$22

96¢

(f)
$5	$5	$1
$1	$1	$5
$1	$1	$5

93¢

$24

70

3. Check (✔) the set with the least amount of money.

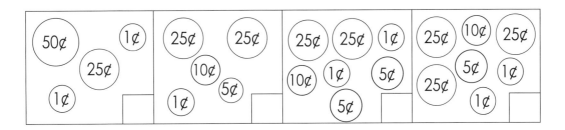

4. Check (✔) the set with the largest amount of money.

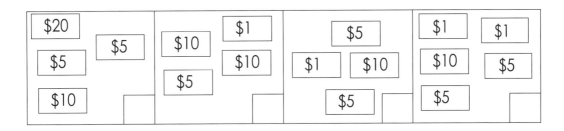

5. Arrange the following sets of money, starting from the largest amount of money.

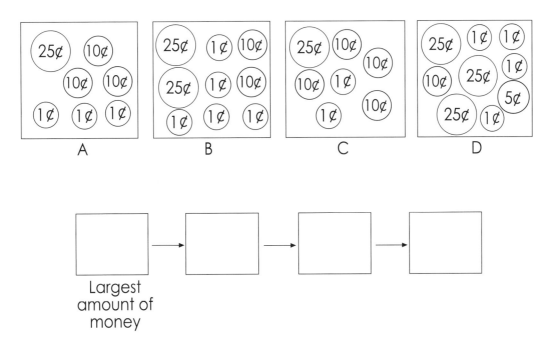

6. Color the correct amount of money needed to buy the items.

(a)

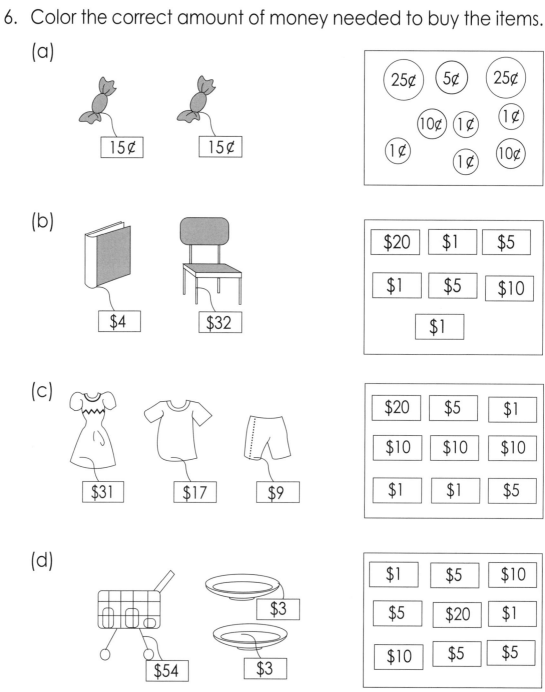

(b)

(c)

(d)

(e)

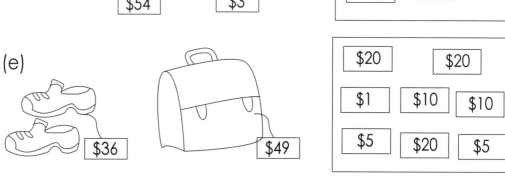

7. Draw more money on the left to buy the items on the right.

(a)
| $1 | $1 | $5 |

$13

(b)
| $10 | $5 | $1 | $1 | $5 |

$38

(c)
| $10 | $10 | $5 | $1 | $1 |

$41

(d)
| $10 | $5 | $1 | $1 | $1 |
| $10 | $1 |

$19 $36

(e)
| $20 | $10 | $20 | $5 | $1 |
| $1 | $1 | $1 |

$31 $45

8. Follow the path. With every correct answer, you earn $2. With every wrong answer, you lose $1. See how much you can earn at the end of the path. Write your answers beside the boxes.

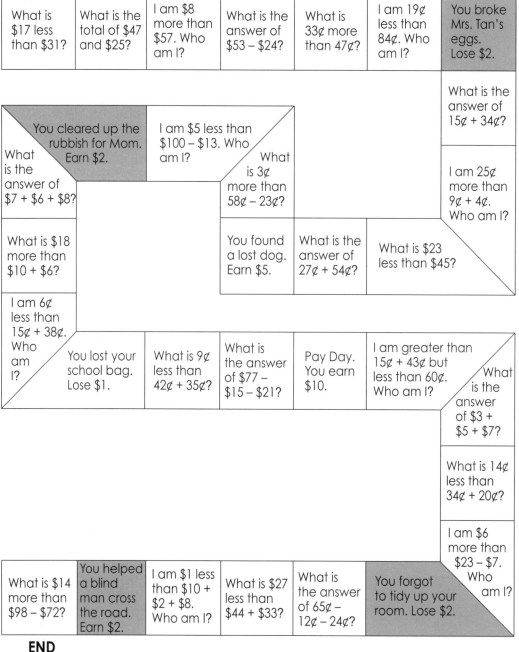

| What is $17 less than $31? | What is the total of $47 and $25? | I am $8 more than $57. Who am I? | What is the answer of $53 – $24? | What is 33¢ more than 47¢? | I am 19¢ less than 84¢. Who am I? | You broke Mrs. Tan's eggs. Lose $2. |

You cleared up the rubbish for Mom. Earn $2.

I am $5 less than $100 – $13. Who am I?

What is the answer of $7 + $6 + $8?

What is 3¢ more than 58¢ – 23¢?

What is the answer of 15¢ + 34¢?

I am 25¢ more than 9¢ + 4¢. Who am I?

What is $18 more than $10 + $6?

You found a lost dog. Earn $5.

What is the answer of 27¢ + 54¢?

What is $23 less than $45?

I am 6¢ less than 15¢ + 38¢. Who am I?

You lost your school bag. Lose $1.

What is 9¢ less than 42¢ + 35¢?

What is the answer of $77 – $15 – $21?

Pay Day. You earn $10.

I am greater than 15¢ + 43¢ but less than 60¢. Who am I?

What is the answer of $3 + $5 + $7?

What is 14¢ less than 34¢ + 20¢?

I am $6 more than $23 – $7. Who am I?

What is $14 more than $98 – $72?

You helped a blind man cross the road. Earn $2.

I am $1 less than $10 + $2 + $8. Who am I?

What is $27 less than $44 + $33?

What is the answer of 65¢ – 12¢ – 24¢?

You forgot to tidy up your room. Lose $2.

END

74

9. Check (✓) the correct statements and cross out (✗) the wrong statements.

   (a) $2 is $14 less than $18.   (   )

   (b) 55 cents more than 27 cents is 83 cents.   (   )

   (c) 17 cents less than 68 cents is 51 cents.   (   )

   (d) 42 cents is 13 cents more than 27 cents.   (   )

   (e) The answer to $1 + $17 + $25 is $47.   (   )

   (f) Take $33 away from $75, the answer is $42.   (   )

   (g) $41 + $29 is larger than $100 – $31.   (   )

   (h) 23¢ + 42¢ is less than 53¢ + 42¢.   (   )

   (i) $13 + $24 is larger than $97 – $18.   (   )

   (j) 97¢ – 25¢ is less than 64¢ + 23¢ but
        larger than 74¢ – 19¢.   (   )

10. Look at the picture. Then fill in the blanks.

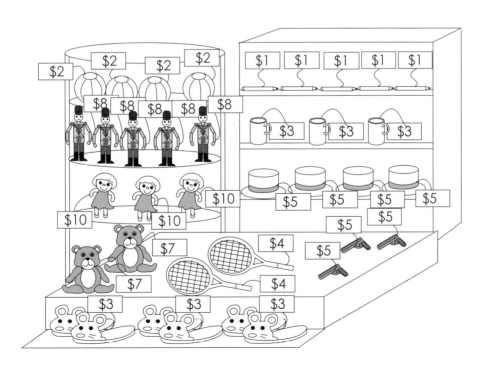

(a) Sharon wants to buy a bear and 2 pairs of bedroom slippers. How much does she need?

She needs _____ .

(b) Terry has $20. He buys a hat and a toy soldier.

(i) How much does he have to pay?

He has to pay _____ .

(ii) How much change will he get?

He will get a change of _____ .

(c) Sean has $43. He wants to buy a ball, a mug and a water pistol.

(i) How much does he need?

He needs _____ .

(ii) Does Sean have enough money to buy these items? Circle the correct answer.
Yes/No

(iii) How much will he have left?

He will have _____ left.

(d) Max buys a racket, a ball and a water pistol. His brother buys a toy soldier, a pencil and a hat.

    (i)   How much does Max have to pay?

        Max has to pay _____ .

    (ii) How much does Max's brother have to pay?

        Max's brother has to pay _____ .

    (iii) How much do they have to pay altogether?

        They have to pay _____ altogether.

    (iv) If Max's mom gives them $70 to spend, how much will they have left?

        They will have _____ left.

(e) Nathan has only $5. He bought 1 item and got a change of $3. What did he buy?

    He bought a _____ .

(f) Mary has $13. She wants to buy 2 dolls. How much more money does she need?

    She needs _____ more.

(g) Paul has $49. He decided to save $34.

    (i)   How much can he spend?

        He can spend _____.

    (ii) Paul wants to buy a water pistol and a bear. How much does he need?

        He needs _____.

    (iii) Does Paul have enough money to buy these items? Circle the correct answer.
         Yes/No

(h) Natalie has $50. She buys a ball and a pair of bedroom slippers. How much change will she get?

    She will get a change of _____ .

11. The picture graph shows the items each child bought from a store.

Fill in the blanks.

(a) (i) How much did Samuel spend?

Samuel spent _____.

(ii) If Samuel had $45, how much would he have left?

Samuel would have _____ left.

(b) (i) Ian and Sara went to the store together. How much did each child spend?

Ian spent _____.

Sara spent _____.

(ii) If Sara had $60, how much change would she get?

Sara would get a change of _____.

(iii) If Ian had $13 left after paying for his items, how much did he have at first?

Ian had _____ at first.

(c) (i)   How much did Candy spend?

Candy spent _____ .

(ii)   If she had $60 at first, how much would she have left?

She would have _____ left.

(d)   If Kelly had $27 left after paying for her items, how much did she have at first?

Kelly had _____ at first.

(e)   Michael needed $11 more to buy all the items he wanted. How much did he have at first?

Michael had _____ at first.

(f)   There are _____ types of items on sale in the store.

(g)   _____ spent $9 less than Ian.

(h)   Candy spent $4 more than _____ .

(i)   _____ and _____ spent the same amount of money.

(j)   _____ spent the least.

(k)   How many items did the children buy altogether?

The children bought _____ items altogether.

WORD PROBLEMS

1. I have $17 less than my brother. My brother has $35. How much do I have?

    □ ○ □ = □

    I have _____.

2. In January, Jason received $8. In February, he received $10. In March, he received $6. How much did Jason receive in all for the three months?

    □ ○ □ ○ □ = □

    Jason received _____ in all for the three months.

3. After paying his brother $34, Rocco had some money left. He used the money to buy a toy car which cost $12. How much money did Rocco have at first?

    □ ○ □ = □

    Rocco had _____ at first.

4. Julie had $85. She gave her sister $7 and bought a book for $12. How much did she have left?

$$\boxed{} \bigcirc \boxed{} = \boxed{}$$

$$\boxed{} \bigcirc \boxed{} = \boxed{}$$

Julie had _____ left.

5. Melissa has a 5-dollar bill, ten dimes and four quarters. After buying a pen for $3 and a big lollipop for $2, how much does she have left?

$$\boxed{} \bigcirc \boxed{} \bigcirc \boxed{} = \boxed{}$$

$$\boxed{} \bigcirc \boxed{} \bigcirc \boxed{} = \boxed{}$$

Melissa has _____ left.

6. Mabel has two 10-dollar bills and six 1-dollar bills. Emily has two 5-dollar bills and five 1-dollar bills.

    (a) Who has more money?

    _____ has more money.

(b) How much more?

$$\boxed{} \bigcirc \boxed{} = \boxed{}$$

_____ more.

7. Ronald had $24. His father gave him $50 for his birthday. With his money, Ronald bought a toy car for $32. How much money did Ronald have left?

$$\boxed{} \bigcirc \boxed{} = \boxed{}$$

$$\boxed{} \bigcirc \boxed{} = \boxed{}$$

Ronald had _____ left.

8. Jimmy had some money. After paying for a toy train with four 5-dollar bills, Jimmy has $14 left. How much did Jimmy have at first?

$$\boxed{} \bigcirc \boxed{} = \boxed{}$$

Jimmy had _____ at first.

Take the Challenge!

The following shows the amount of money Catherine has. After spending $37, does she still have enough money to buy the two items shown on the right?

$20	$20	$10
$5	$5	$20
$1	$1	$1

$17

$10

Circle the correct answer.

Yes/No

If yes, how much money does she have left after buying the two items?

She has _____ left after buying the two items.

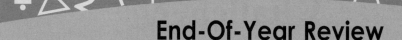

End-Of-Year Review

1. Circle the one which gives 13.

    13 + 1   15 − 4   16 − 3   17 + 2   19 − 7

2. Look at the diagram and answer the questions.

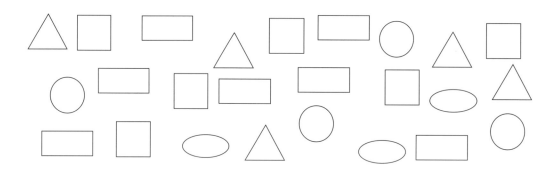

(a) There are _____ rectangles.

(b) There are _____ more squares than ovals.

(c) There are _____ circles fewer than rectangles.

(d) There are _____ triangles, ovals and squares altogether.

3. Color the loaf of bread that is 4th from the right.

4. Look at the diagram and answer the questions.

(a) Rod C is _____  long.

(b) Rod A is shorter than Rod _____ but longer than Rod

_____ .

(c) Rod _____ is the longest.

5. Fill in the missing number in each pattern.

(a)

  33   35   39

(b)

 90   87       81

6. Check (✓) the one that gives the largest answer.

3 tens 2 ones – 7	40 – 10	29 + 7	2 tens 3 ones + 10 ones	38 – 9

7. $19 - 7 = \boxed{} - 8$

8. Complete the pattern by drawing the missing figure.

9. This graph shows the favorite activities of some children. Each ◯ stands for 1 child. Fill in the correct answers.

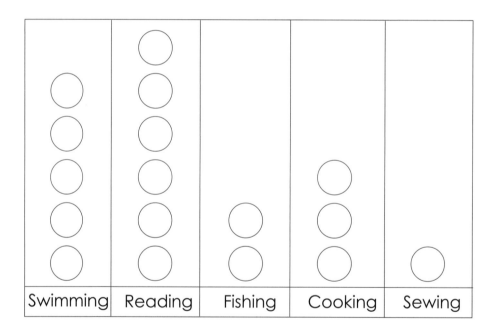

(a) There are _____ children who like reading.

(b) _____ children like swimming more than cooking.

(c) Four fewer children like fishing than _____.

(d) There are _____ children altogether.

10. Circle the correct one that matches the picture.

2×5 $5 + 5 + 5$ 3×3 5×3 $3 + 3 + 3$ 2×3

11. 14 more than 3 is _____ .

12. Circle the number of marbles to be put equally into 4 bottles.

13. Check (✓) the clock which shows 'half past 5'.

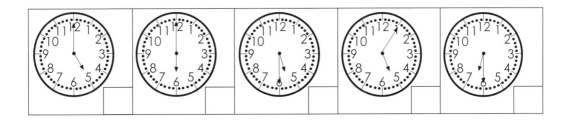

14. Arrange the numbers, starting from the smallest.

29	2 tens 1 one	thirty-five	17	3 tens 7 ones

Smallest

89

15. Write an addition sentence and a multiplication sentence for this picture.

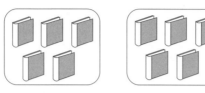 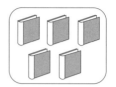

(a) ☐ + ☐ + ☐ = ☐

(b) ☐ × ☐ = ☐

16.

How many stars must Lisa give to Aaron so that they share the same number of stars? _____

17. Count and write the correct amount of money in the box.

18. Look at the diagram and answer the questions.

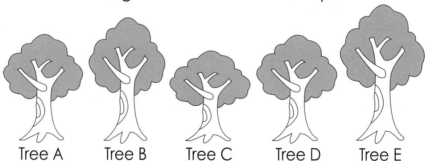

(a) Tree B is shorter than Tree _____.

(b) Tree _____ is as tall as Tree _____.

(c) Tree _____ is the tallest.

(d) Tree _____ is the shortest.

90

19. Circle the two of the following which give the same answer.

   31 + 7   40 – 3   27 + 9   30 + 9   29 + 8

20. 6 tens 7 ones = 5 tens + _____ ones

21. Write the following in words.

   (a) 1st _____   (b) 9th _____

   (c) 40 _____   (d) 38 _____

22. Cara ate 5 pieces of candy.
    Pamela ate 2 fewer pieces of candy than Cara.
    Tim ate 3 more pieces of candy than Pamela.
    Sophie ate 4 fewer pieces of candy than Tim.

    Complete the picture graph to show the number of pieces of

    candy each child ate. Each 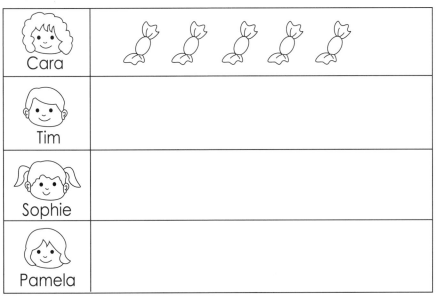 stands for 1 piece.

23. If $\triangle$ + $\triangle$ = 18, what number does $\triangle$ stand for?

   $\triangle$ = _____

24. Arrange the numbers, starting from the largest.

49	5 tens 0 ones	74	90 ones	eighty-six

Largest

25. There are some pieces of candy to be given to 3 boys equally. Circle the number of pieces of candy to be given to each boy.

26. Color 2 bricks to make up 16.

7	2	8	9	11	3

27. Fill in the blank with "heavier", "the heaviest", "lighter" or "the lightest".

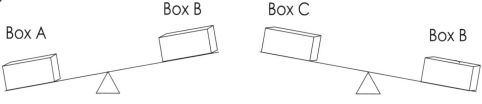

Box A is _____ box.

28. $7 + \boxed{} = 17$

29. $\boxed{} - 4 = 10$

30. Color to make $57.

$10	$5	$1	$10

$5	$10	$1	$1

$20	$1

31. There are 19 children in the class. The picture graph shows the favorite subject of the children. Each ⬤ stands for 1 child. Complete the picture graph by drawing the circles for Mathematics.

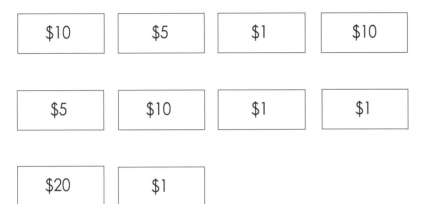

32. Mark is 5th in line. There are 11 children in line after him. How many children are in line?

There are _____ children in line.

33. 63 − 9 = ☐

34. Fill in the missing number in the pattern.

| 44 | 46 | 48 | | 52 | 54 |

35. James has $72. After buying the
     items on the right, how much
     does he have left?

     James has _____ left.

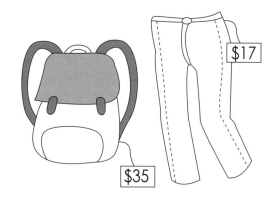

$17

$35

36. Draw the correct number of  in each circle to show 5 x 4.
     Then fill in the missing number in the box.

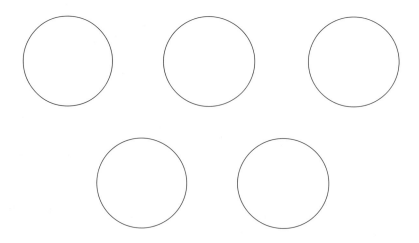

5 × 4 = ☐

37. Write the correct time shown on the clock.

(a)

(b)

38. 2 tens 5 ones less than 7 tens is _____ tens _____ ones.

39. Fill in the missing number in the pattern.

| 90 | 80 | 70 | | 50 | 40 |

40. Circle the two of the following which give the same answer.

73 – 4   49 + 19   55 + 7   81 – 7   54 + 14

PART 2

41. Susie bought 37 ping pong balls. Eleven were dented while she was playing ping pong. She threw the dented ones away. How many good ping pong balls did she have left?

 ○ = ☐

Susie had _____ ping pong balls left.

42. Aunt Lina bought 2 boxes of cakes. One box had 21 cakes. The other box had 13 cakes. How many cakes did Aunt Lina buy altogether?

$$\boxed{} \bigcirc \boxed{} = \boxed{}$$

Aunt Lina bought _____ cakes altogether.

43. A tray contains 6 cookies. How many cookies are there on 3 such trays?

$$\boxed{} \bigcirc \boxed{} = \boxed{}$$

There are _____ cookies on 3 such trays.

44. Cindy has 7 sweaters. Jenny has 8 sweaters. Queenie has 5 sweaters. How many sweaters do they have altogether?

$$\boxed{} \bigcirc \boxed{} \bigcirc \boxed{} = \boxed{}$$

They have _____ sweaters altogether.

45. Anne buys a bag for $5 and a pair of shoes for $9. She has $8 left now. How much money does she have at first?

$$\boxed{} \bigcirc \boxed{} \bigcirc \boxed{} = \boxed{}$$

Anne has _____ at first.

46. Each child at a party receives 3 pieces of candy. There are 18 pieces of candy. How many children are there at the party?

There are _____ children at the party.

47. Mom fried 90 chicken wings for a party. After the party, there were only 25 chicken wings left. How many chicken wings were eaten at the party?

□ ○ □ = □

_____ chicken wings were eaten at the party.

48. Janet had 18 stamps. She gave 5 stamps to her sister. She also gave some stamps to her brother. She had 6 stamps left. How many stamps did she give to her brother?

□ ○ □ = □

□ ○ □ = □

Janet gave _____ stamps to her brother.

49. There were 3 pieces of candy in each box. Sandra gave 2 boxes of candy to each of her 2 friends. How many pieces of candy did Sandra give away?

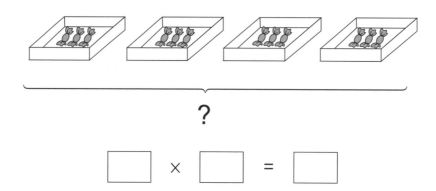

Sandra gave away _____ pieces of candy.

50. Kym, Adrian and Colin bought 9 books each. How many books did they buy altogether?

They bought _____ books altogether.

More Challenging Problems

1. In a line, Sean is 3rd from the front and 4th from the end. How many people are in line?

   There are _____ people in line.

2. Mrs. Lim has the following coins in her coin purse.

   10¢ 25¢ 10¢ 5¢ 1¢ 1¢ 1¢
   10¢ 10¢ 25¢ 1¢ 1¢ 10¢ 10¢

   She wants to divide and give the money equally to her two children. How much money will each child get? Draw the coins each child will receive.

   Each child will receive _____ cents.

3. How many  does the book weigh?

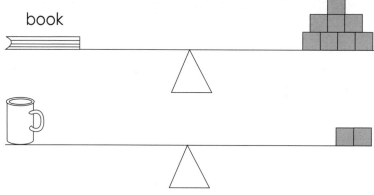

The book weighs about _____ 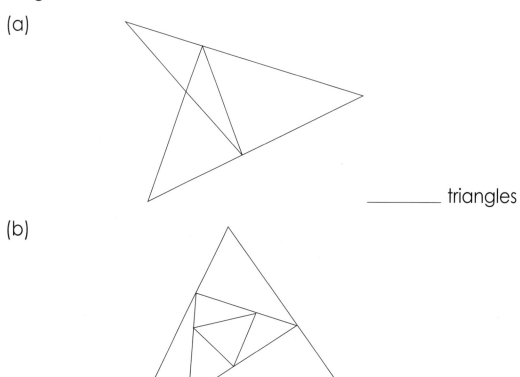 .

4. How many triangles are there in each of the following diagrams?

(a)

_____ triangles

(b)

_____ triangles

(c)

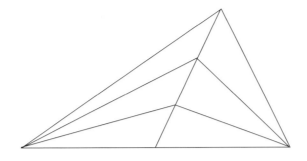

_____ triangles

5. (a) Ryan is 6 years younger than his cousin, Danny. Danny is 13 years old. How old will Ryan be 8 years from now?

Eight years from now, Ryan will be _____ years old.

(b) Felix is 7 years older than his sister, Rose. Rose is 8 years old. How old will Felix be 6 years from now?

Six years from now, Felix will be _____ years old.

(c) Mr. Johnson has three children. One of them is an 11-year-old girl. The other two are twin boys. If the sum of the ages of the three children is 29, how old are the twins?

The twins are each _____ years old.

6. Fill in the numbers 1, 3, 5, 7 and 9 in the squares so that each total of the three numbers in the horizontal and vertical positions is 15. Each number can only be used once.

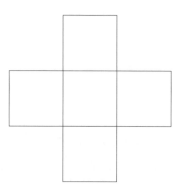

7. Complete the pattern in the last box.

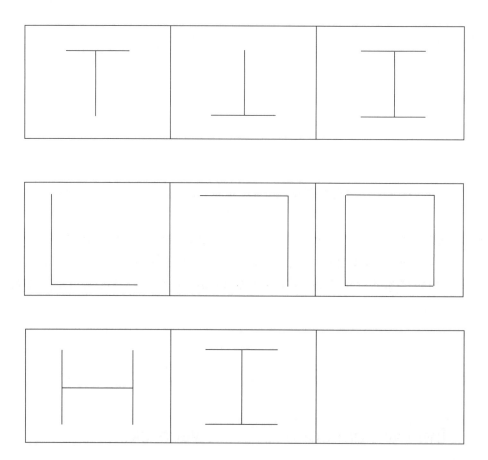

8. In each of the following diagrams, the total for each row and column is given. Can you work out the numbers, not including zeros, to be placed in the figures?

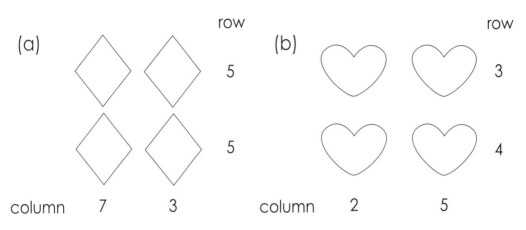

(a)

row
5
5

column   7   3

(b)

row
3
4

column   2   5

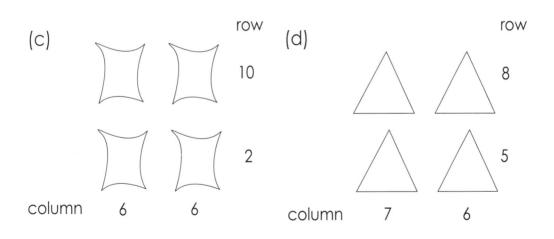

(c)

row
10
2

column   6   6

(d)

row
8
5

column   7   6

9. Fill in the numbers 1, 2, 3, 4, 5, 6, 7 and 8 in the circles to make the total of the four numbers on each of the two rings and on each of the two lines 18.

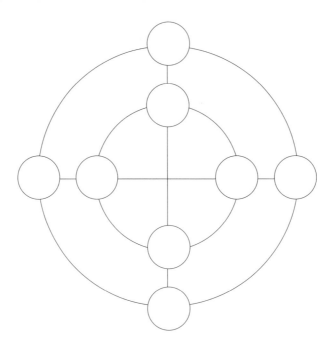

10. Fill in the 9 boxes with 3 ones, 3 twos, and 3 threes so that the numbers in any row, column or diagonal line have the same total. Each of the 9 numbers can only be used once.

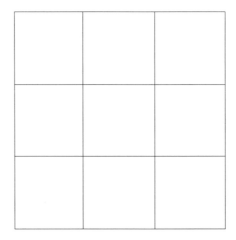

11. Complete the pattern in this figure by drawing the correct shapes in the empty squares.

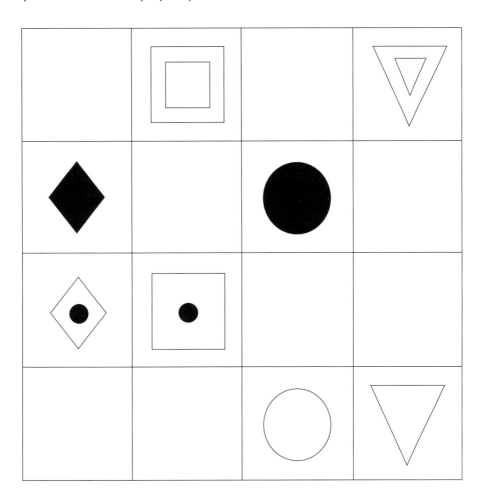

12. (a) If this clock is half an hour slower than the actual time, find the actual time.

The actual time is _____.

(b) If this clock is 1 hour faster than the actual time, find the actual time.

The actual time is _____.

Answers

Topic 1: Comparing Numbers

1. (a) 2, chicks, frogs
   (b) 3, sea horses, crabs
   (c) 7, bananas, cherries
2. (a) 6   (b) 8
   (c) 11   (d) 10
   (e) 12   (f) 6
   (g) 12   (h) 0
   (i) 12
3. (a) 8   (b) 6
   (c) 13   (d) largest

Word Problems

1. 15
2. 9
3. (a) 2   (b) 12

Take the Challenge!

1. (a) 4   (b) 5
   (c) 2   (d) 2
   (e) apples, 2
2. 14

Topic 2: Picture Graphs

1. (a) 8   (b) 6
   (c) 4   (d) 4
   (e) lettuce
   (f) carrot, tomato, broccoli, lettuce
2. (a) 8   (b) 9
   (c) 11   (d) 7
   (e) 6   (f) hamsters
   (g) dogs   (h) 6
   (i) 19
3. (a) 12   (b) 7
   (c) 7   (d) 9
   (e) toy cars   (f) marbles
   (g) 5
4. (a) 15   (b) 7
   (c) 5   (d) 4
   (e) caramel swirl
   (f) chocolate fudge
   (g) 20

5. (a)

Stamps	Stickers	Coins	Seashells

   (b) 3

Take the Challenge!

(a) 20   (b) 12
(c) 5   (d) 11
(e) 15   (f) 18
(g) 20   (h) 8
(i) strawberries   (j) cherries
(k) tomatoes   (l) papayas
(m) watermelons
(n) apples or oranges
(o) 20   p) 16
(q) 13   (r) 8

Topic 3: Numbers to 40

1. (a) 29   (b) 34
   (c) 25   (d) 40
2. (a)

   (b)

   (c)

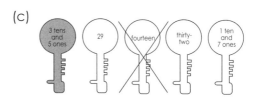

(d)

(e)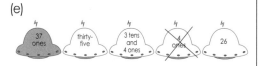

3. (a) 23 + 14 = 37   (b) 19 + 17 = 36

(c) 27 + 11 = 38

4. (a) 24   (b) 31
   (c) 35   (d) 24
   (e) 39   (f) 28
   (g) 27   (h) 37

5. (a) 22 + 6 = 28   (b) 31 + 8 = 39

   (c) 25 + 9 = 34   (d) 5 + 26 = 31

   (e) 29 + 7 = 36   (f) 27 + 8 = 35

   (g) 36 + 4 = 40   (h) 6 + 28 = 34

6.

8. (a) 35   (b) 21
   (c) 16   (d) 24
   (e) 28   (f) 23
   (g) 18   (h) 37

9. (a) 25 − 3 = 22   (b) 39 − 5 = 34
   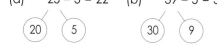

   (c) 23 − 8 = 15   (d) 32 − 7 = 25

   (e) 40 − 9 = 31   (f) 37 − 6 = 31

   (g) 28 − 7 = 21   (h) 24 − 9 = 15

10. (b)   (c)
    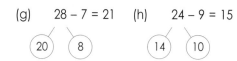

    (d)   (e)
    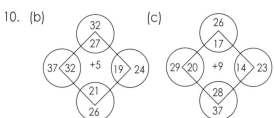

    (f)   (g)
    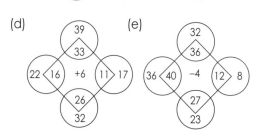

    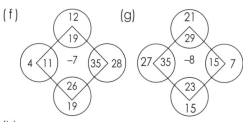

    (h)
    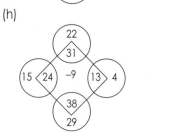

11. (a) ✗ (b) ✓
    (c) ✗ (d) ✓
    (e) ✗ (f) ✗
    (g) ✓ (h) ✗
    (i) ✗ (j) ✓

Word Problems

1. 25 – 7 = 18, 18

2. 31 + 5 = 36, 36

3. 37 – 8 = 29, 29

4. 19 + 6 + 8 = 33, 33

5. 34 – 28 = 6, 6

6. (a) B (b) 31 – 23 = 8, 8

7. 26 – 5 – 8 = 13, 13
8. 10 + 9 = 19, 19
9. 18 + 2 + 7 = 27, 27

Take the Challenge!

1. (a) A = 24, B = 22 (b) C = 38
2. ▽ = 6, □ = 3

Topic 4: Multiplication

1. (a) 5 + 5 + 5 + 5 = 20
       4 × 5 = 20
   (b) 3 + 3 + 3 + 3 +
       3 = 15
       5 × 3 = 15
   (c) 8 + 8 + 8 + 8 = 32
       4 × 8 = 32

(d) 7 + 7 + 7 = 21
    3 × 7 = 21
(e) 5 + 5 + 5 = 15
    3 × 5 = 15

2.

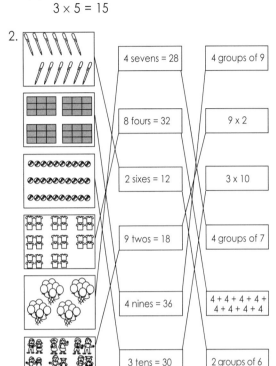

3. (a) 4 × 6 = 24 (b) 6 × 2 = 12
   (c) 4 × 4 = 16 (d) 3 × 9 = 27
   (e) 7 × 4 = 28

4.

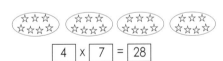

5.

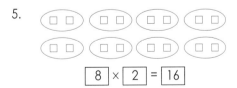

6.

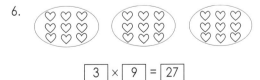

7.

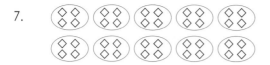

$$\boxed{10} \times \boxed{4} = \boxed{40}$$

8.

$$\boxed{7} \times \boxed{5} = \boxed{35}$$

9. (a) ✗   (b) ✗
   (c) ✓   (d) ✗
   (e) ✓   (f) ✓
   (g) ✗   (h) ✗
   (i) ✗   (j) ✓
10. (a) 16, 18, 20   (b) 20
    (c) 40   (d) 30, 27
    (e) 24

Word Problems
1. $4 \times 8 = 32$, 32
2. $6 \times 3 = 18$, 18
3. $5 \times 6 = 30$, 30
4. (a) 5   (b) 4
   (c) 20
5. $3 \times 7 = 21$, $2 \times 7 = 14$, $21 + 14 = 35$, 35
6. $3 \times 10 = 30$, $30 - 7 = 23$, 23
7. $7 \times 2 = 14$, 14
8. (a) $6 \times 5 = 30$, 30   (b) $30 - 8 = 22$, 22

Take the Challenge!
(a) greater than
(b) less than, greater than
(c) the same as
(d) the same as, greater than
(e) greater than

Topic 5: Division
1. (a)  , 4

   (b) , 3

   (c) , 8

(d)  , 2

2. (a) , 3

   (b)  , 5

   (c) , 2

   (d) 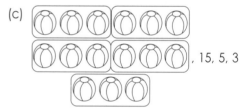 , 6

3. (a) , 20, 5, 4

   (b) , 14, 7, 2

   (c) , 15, 5, 3

4. (a) , 16, 4, 4

   (b) , 18, 6, 3

   (c) , 15, 3, 5

Word Problems
1. 5   2. 4   3. 2
4. 6   5. 4   6. 2
7. 5   8. 7

Take the Challenge!
1. 9
2. Draw 6 more oranges.

110

Topic 6: Time

1. (a) — Half past 8
   (b) — Half past 2
   (c) — 9 o'clock
   (d) — Half past 1
   (e) — 5 o'clock
   (f) — 11 o'clock

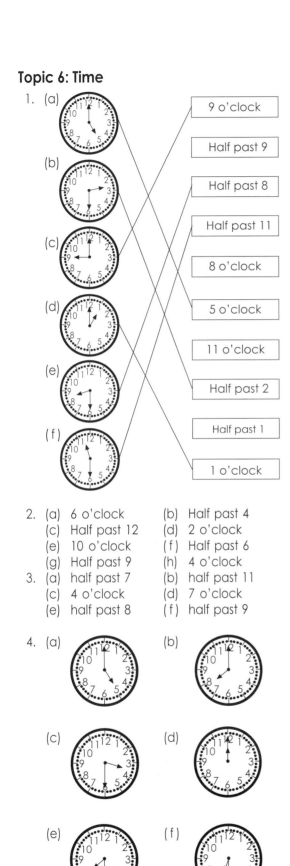

9 o'clock

Half past 9

Half past 8

Half past 11

8 o'clock

5 o'clock

11 o'clock

Half past 2

Half past 1

1 o'clock

2. (a) 6 o'clock   (b) Half past 4
   (c) Half past 12   (d) 2 o'clock
   (e) 10 o'clock   (f) Half past 6
   (g) Half past 9   (h) 4 o'clock

3. (a) half past 7   (b) half past 11
   (c) 4 o'clock   (d) 7 o'clock
   (e) half past 8   (f) half past 9

4. (a)   (b)   (c)   (d)   (e)   (f)

5. (a)   (b)
   (c)   (d)
   (e)   (f)

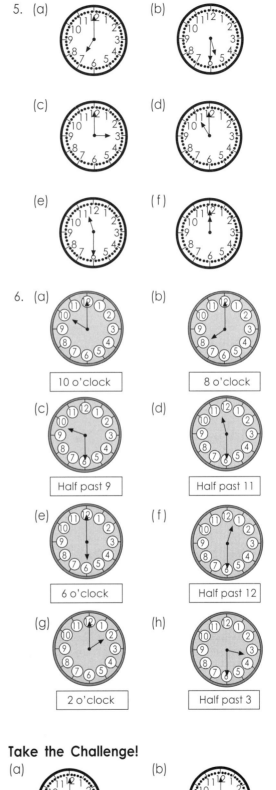

6. (a)   (b)

   10 o'clock   8 o'clock

   (c)   (d)

   Half past 9   Half past 11

   (e)   (f)

   6 o'clock   Half past 12

   (g)   (h)

   2 o'clock   Half past 3

Take the Challenge!

(a)   (b)

111

(c)   (d)

(e)

Topic 7: Numbers to 100

1. (a) fifty-three   (b) seventy-seven
   (c) eighty-six   (d) ninety-four
2. (a) 46   (b) 73   (c) 4, 9
   (d) 8, 5   (e) 90   (f) 3, 8
   (g) 54   (h) 1, 5, 15   (i) 9
   (j) 90   (k) 3   (l) 30
3.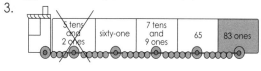
4.
5.
6. (a) 47   (b) 57   (c) 86   (d) 68
   (e) 75   (f) 86   (g) 74   (h) 71
   (i) 69   (j) 98
7. (a) $63 + 6 = 69$ (b) $85 + 8 = 93$
   (60) (3)   (5) (3)

   (c) $72 + 7 = 79$ (d) $9 + 55 = 64$
   (70) (2)   (4) (5)

   (e) $44 + 6 = 50$ (f) $5 + 92 = 97$
   (40) (4)   (2) (90)

   (g) $57 + 4 = 61$ (h) $81 + 7 = 88$
   (3) (1)   (80) (1)

   (i) $68 + 6 = 74$ (j) $8 + 75 = 83$
   (2) (4)   (3) (5)

8. (a) $45 + 50 = 95$ (b) $33 + 60 = 93$
   (5) (40)   (3) (30)

   (c) $79 + 20 = 99$ (d) $56 + 30 = 86$
   (9) (70)   (6) (50)

   (e) $40 + 27 = 67$ (f) $48 + 40 = 88$
   (20) (7)   (8) (40)

9. (a) $24 + \quad 63 = 87$
   (60) (3)

   (b) $18 + \quad 57 = 75$
   (50) (7)

   (c) $49 + \quad 26 = 75$
   (20) (6)

   (d) $35 + \quad 12 = 47$
   (10) (2)

   (e) $71 + \quad 13 = 84$
   (10) (3)

   (f) $38 + \quad 42 = 80$
   (40) (2)

   (g) $26 + \quad 51 = 77$
   (50) (1)

   (h) $65 + \quad 19 = 84$
   (10) (9)

   (i) $66 + \quad 17 = 83$
   (10) (7)

(j) 34 + 22 = 56

10. (a)

(b)

(c)
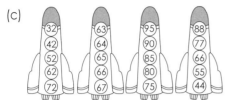

(d)

11. (a) 48   (b) 78   (c) 38   (d) 65
    (e) 58   (f) 57   (g) 47   (h) 55
    (i) 37   (j) 13

12. (a)   58 – 6 = 52   (b)   75 – 3 = 72
         50   8   70   5

    (c)   61 – 7 = 54   (d)   43 – 5 = 38
         51   10   33   10

    (e)   89 – 8 = 81   (f)   62 – 6 = 56
         80   9   52   10

    (g)   80 – 9 = 71   (h)   59 – 5 = 54
         70   10   50   9

    (i)   77 – 8 = 69   (j)   96 – 4 = 92
         67   10   90   6

13. (a)   46 – 20 = 26   (b)   59 – 40 = 19
         6   40   9   50

    (c)   85 – 30 = 55   (d)   67 – 50 = 17
         5   80   7   60

(e)   93 – 40 = 53   (f)   71 – 20 = 51
     3   90   1   70

14. (a)   68 – 35 = 33
         30   5

    (b)   75 – 24 = 51
         20   4

    (c)   94 – 18 = 76
         10   8

    (d)   49 – 27 = 22
         20   7

    (e)   60 – 15 = 45
         10   5

    (f)   51 – 16 = 35
         10   6

    (g)   83 – 47 = 36
         40   7

    (h)   57 – 49 = 8
         40   9

    (i)   77 – 31 = 46
         30   1

    (j)   86 – 22 = 64
         20   2

15. (a) ✓   (b) ✗   (c) ✗
    (d) ✓   (e) ✗   (f) ✓
    (g) ✗   (h) ✗   (i) ✗

Word Problems
1. 38 + 17 = 55, 55
2. 57 – 14 = 43, 43 – 19 = 24, 24
3. 25 + 17 = 42, 42 + 25 = 67, 67
4. 44 – 15 = 29, 29 + 23 = 52, 52
5. 42 – 19 = 23, 23
6. 43 + 8 = 51, 51

7. (a) $57 - 38 = 19, 19$ (b) $57 + 38 = 95, 95$
8. $30 + 25 = 55, 55$

Take the Challenge!
1. $68 = 6$ tens 8 ones
       $= 5$ tens 18 ones
       $= 4$ tens 28 ones
       $= 3$ tens 38 ones
       $= 2$ tens 48 ones
       $= 1$ ten 58 ones
2. (a) The sum of all the four numbers in each box is 100.
        The missing number is 10.
    (b)
    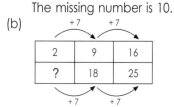

       (Note that the bottom number subtract the top number in each column is 9.)
       The missing number is 11.

Topic 8: Money
1. (a) 2   (b) 25   (c) 5   (d) 10
    (e) 5   (f) 10   (g) 2   (h) 2
    (i) 4   (j) 10

2. (a)
    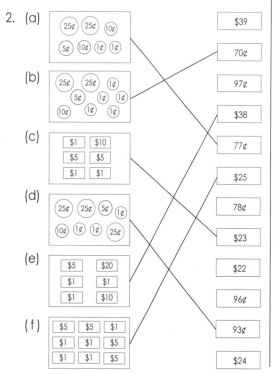

3.

4.
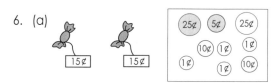

5. D → B → C → A

6. (a)

    (b)
    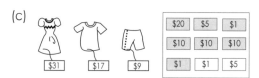

    (c)
    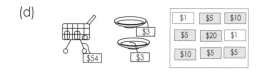

    (d)

    (e)
    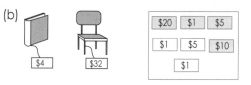

7. (a) | $5 | $1 |

    (b) | $10 | $5 | $1 |

    (c) | $10 | $1 | $1 | $1 | $1 |

    (d) | $20 | $5 | $1 |

    (e) | $10 | $5 | $1 | $1 |

114

8.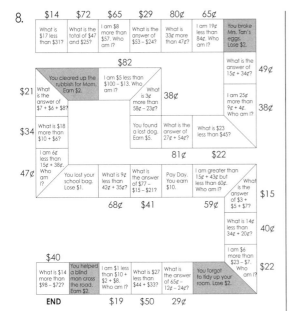

9. (a) ✗   (b) ✗
   (c) ✓   (d) ✗
   (e) ✗   (f) ✓
   (g) ✓   (h) ✓
   (i) ✗   (j) ✓

10. (a) $13
   (b) (i) $13   (ii) $7
   (c) (i) $10   (ii) Yes   (iii) $33
   (d) (i) $11   (ii) $14
       (iii) $25   (iv) $45
   (e) ball   (f) $7
   (g) (i) $15   (ii) $12   (iii) Yes
   (h) $45

11. (a) (i) $16   (ii) $29
   (b) (i) $25, $23 (ii) $37   (iii) $38
   (c) (i) $25   (ii) $35
   (d) $48   (e) $6
   (f) 12   (g) Samuel
   (h) Kelly   (i) Ian, Candy
   (j) Samuel   (k) 18

Word Problems

1. 35 − 17 = 18, $18   2. 8 + 10 + 6 = 24, $24
3. 12 + 34 = 46, $46
4. 85 − 7 = 78,
   78 − 12 = 66, $66
5. 5 + 1 + 1 = 7
   7 − 3 − 2 = 2, $2
6. (a) Mabel   (b) 26 − 15 = 11, $11
7. 24 + 50 = 74,
   74 − 32 = 42, $42
8. 20 + 14 = 34, $34

Take the Challenge!
Yes, $19

End-of-Year Review

Part 1

1. 16 − 3
2. (a) 7   (b) 3
   (c) 3   (d) 14
3.
4. (a) 5   (b) B, C
   (c) B
5. (a) 37   (b) 84
6.

3 tens 2 ones − 7	40 − 10	29 + 7	2 tens 3 ones + 10 ones	38 − 9
		✓		

7. 20   8.

9. (a) 6   (b) 2
   (c) reading   (d) 17
10. 2 × 5   5 + 5 + 5   (3 × 3)   5 × 3   (3 + 3 + 3)   2 × 3
11. 17
12.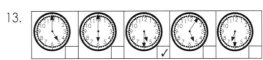
13.
14.

17	2 tens 1 one	29	thirty-five	3 tens 7 ones

15. (a) 5 + 5 + 5 = 15   (b) 3 × 5 = 15
16. 3   17. 88¢
18. (a) E   (b) A, D
   (c) E   (d) C
19. 31 + 7   (40 − 3)   27 + 9   30 + 9   (29 + 8)
20. 17
21. (a) first   (b) ninth
   (c) forty   (d) thirty-eight
22.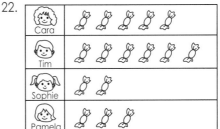

23. 9

24.

90 ones	eighty-six	74	5 tens 0 ones	49

25.

26.

7	2	8	9	11	3

27. the heaviest
28. 10   29. 14

30.

$10	$5	$1	$10
$5	$10	$1	$1
$20	$1		

31.

English	● ● ● ● ●
Music	● ● ● ● ● ● ●
Mathematics	● ● ●
Art	● ● ● ● ●

32. 16   33. 54
34. 50   35. $20

36.

$$5 \times 4 = 20$$

37. (a) 2 o'clock
    (b) half past 9
38. 4, 5
39. 60
40. 73 – 4 (49 + 19)   55 + 7   81 – 7   (54 + 14)

Part 2
41. 37 – 11 = 26, 26
42. 21 + 13 = 34, 34
43. 3 × 6 = 18, 18
44. 7 + 8 + 5 = 20, 20
45. 5 + 9 + 8 = 22, $22
46. 6
47. 90 – 25 = 65, 65
48. 18 – 5 = 13, 13 – 6 = 7, 7
49. 4 × 3 = 12, 12
50. 9 + 9 + 9 = 27, 27

More Challenging Problems
1.

There are 6 people in line.

2. Each child will receive 60 cents.

3. The book weighs about 4 ☕.
4. (a) 8   (b) 9   (c) 15
5. (a) Ravi's age now = 13 – 6 = 7
        Ravi's age 8 years from now
        = 7 + 8 = 15
        Eight years from now, Ravi will be
        15 years old.
   (b) Felix's age now = 8 + 7 = 15
        Felix's age 6 years from now
        15 + 6 = 21
        Six years from now, Felix will be
        21 years old.
   (c) Sum of the ages of the twin boys
        = 29 – 11 = 18
        The twins are each 9 years old.
6. One possible way is

	3	
1	5	9
	7	

7.

8. (a) 4 1   or   3 2
        3 2   4 1
   (b) 1 2
        1 3
   (c) 5 5
        1 1
   (d) Possible answers:
        4 4   or   6 2
        3 2   1 4
    or 5 3   or   3 5
        2 3   4 1

9.

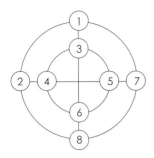

10.

3	1	2
1	2	3
2	3	1

11.

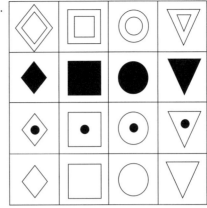

12. (a) 5 o'clock
    (b) 7 o'clock